I SAILED TO ZION

I SAILED TO ZION

True Stories of Young Pioneers
Who Crossed the Oceans

———— • —— • ————

Susan Arrington Madsen and Fred E. Woods

———— • —— • ————

CINNAMON
TREE

Published by
Deseret Book Company
Salt Lake City, Utah

FOR OUR CHILDREN

Emily & David, Rebecca, Sarah, and Rachel

—SM

Samuel, Daniel, Addie, Freddy, and Shirley Ann

—FEW

Library of Congress Cataloging-in-Publication Data

Madsen, Susan Arrington.
  I sailed to Zion : true stories of young pioneers who crossed the ocean / Susan Arrington Madsen & Fred E. Woods.
    p. cm.
  Includes bibliographical references and index.
  ISBN 1–57345–651–9
  1. Mormon youth–Biography. 2. Mormon children–Biography. 3. Teenage immigrants–United States–Biography. 4. Immigrant children–Religious aspects–Church of Jesus Christ of Latter-day Saints. 6. Mormon converts–Biography. I. Woods, Fred E. II. Title.

  BX8643.Y6 M33 2000
  289.3'32'08691–dc21   00-023599

Printed in the United States of America   72082-6643

10   9   8   7   6   5   4   3   2   1

"SAVE US, O GOD.

THINE OCEAN IS SO LARGE,

AND OUR LITTLE BOAT

IS SO SMALL."

—A SEA VOYAGER'S PRAYER

Preface

Many books have been written about the epic story of the Mormon pioneers who crossed the Plains between 1847 and 1869 and settled the Great Basin Kingdom of the West. Much attention has rightfully been paid to those determined souls who braved sickness, unpredictable weather, accidents, wild animals, and physical exhaustion to find religious freedom in the unsettled deserts of the Utah Territory.

However, while focusing most of our attention on the experiences of the overland travelers, we may have missed—so to speak—the boat. Most new converts to Mormonism who began the long trek across the Plains had recently come to America from lands far across the ocean. Before taking their first steps toward Zion, most of them had spent from ten days to ten weeks on a sailing ship or steamer on the oceans to gather to America.

This book takes a look at nineteenth-century ocean immigration through the eyes of Mormon children and teenagers who experienced the excitement and trials of being on a ship for days, weeks, and, in some cases, months.

What was it like to be out in the middle of a vast ocean for so long? What was it like to watch someone being buried at sea? What did the drinking water taste like after it had been sitting in a wooden barrel for a month? And what was it like to huddle together below deck during a violent thunderstorm?

To answer these and other questions, and to capture the power of personal experience, we have chosen to include in this book only first-person accounts. Who can better describe waving good-bye to mother and father at the port of Liverpool than the young man who stood alone onboard as the ship departed, trying to hide his tears? Who can better write of the thrill of seeing America for the first time than the little girl who would not forget that moment for the rest of her life?

In preparing this book, we have studied hundreds of such personal records. Most of the accounts we examined were written years after the experiences occurred—very few children or teenagers managed to keep a journal as the ship heaved and sighed on the ocean waves.

This book contains two kinds of excerpts. First, there are longer reminiscences that describe the youthful experiences of the writers. These narratives make up the bulk of the book. Second, there are many shorter excerpts that enrich and complement the longer narratives. These shorter excerpts tell a single incident or make an observation that add detail and color to our understanding of pioneer ocean travel. The shorter excerpts appear as sidebars throughout the book.

Because many of the young women who sailed to America are better known by their married names than by their maiden names, we have included their married names in parentheses in the chapter titles.

For readability, we have standardized spelling and most punctuation. We have occasionally changed wording, but only when necessary to clarify meaning. We have also deleted sentences and phrases in places not critical to the actual narrative, especially in longer chapters. Narrative material has sometimes been reordered to render a more chronological telling of events. In some cases narratives have been combined from more than one source.

For the most part, these excerpts recount only the portion of the histories that deal with the actual voyage to America. For those desiring to read more about a particular pioneer, the title and location of the original history has been provided at the end of each chapter.

Readers may be interested in the difference between the words *emigrate/*

immigrate and *emigrant/immigrant*. To emigrate is to leave one's country of native origin to go to a new land. To immigrate is to arive in a new land from one's native country. In this book, we have used the terms according to their definition in all new written material. However, we have left the words as they originally appeared in all first person accounts.

Many people have helped make this book possible. We are deeply indebted to the late Conway B. Sonne for his pioneering research on nineteenth-century Mormon maritime migration. His publications have become standard references for those wanting to know more about this important part of Latter-day Saint history.

We are grateful to the staff of the Library and Archives of the Historical Department of The Church of Jesus Christ of Latter-day Saints in Salt Lake City. We are especially grateful to Melvin L. Bashore and Linda L. Haslam, who prepared *Mormons on the High Seas: Ocean Voyage Narratives to America (1840–1890)*. We appreciate the assistance of William W. Slaughter, photograph archivist.

Ann Buttars and her associates in the Special Collections and Archives at the Utah State University Merrill Library were generous with their time and resources. We have also benefitted from the refining suggestions of Brigham Young University Faculty Editing Services, Don Norton, director.

We are indebted to descendants of those whose stories are told in this book for providing family histories and valuable photographs. They include Renae Chase, Janice Francom, Lois Lazenby, Sylvia S. Sharp, Thelma Anderson, Clarice Porter, Marilyn H. Mecham, Max Groom, Barbara Whiting, Jan Stock, LaPriel Tobler, Sheryl Kempton, Barbara K. Anderson, Rohn Brown, Max Wheelwright, Mona Lowe, George D. Hulse, Ella Mae Groom Hinckley, Scott Hansen, Vernon Anthony, Reed Zaugg, Noel Zaugg, Marlene Havertz, Barbara Judd, Linda Ferney, Orpha Mohr, Audrey Chappell, Eva Fay Anderson, Daina Zollinger, and the late Paul Ahlstrom. Information on individual photographs and illustrations is found at the back of the book.

Our eternal companions, Dean and JoAnna, have been constantly supportive and have spent long hours reading our manuscript and making helpful editing suggestions.

We have enjoyed this project. We now have a much greater understanding of the hardships endured by these young Latter-day Saints and a much greater appreciation for their faith, courage, and heroic desire to live with the Saints in

"Zion." Their writings have caused us to marvel, to weep, and to rejoice with them as they fulfilled their loftiest dreams: they gathered to the promised land, they established eternal families, and they helped build the kingdom of God.

Susan Arrington Madsen
Fred E. Woods
July 2000

Valborg Rasmussen

Introduction

Valborg Rasmussen was thirteen years old in 1888 when she kissed her widowed mother good-bye at their home in Copenhagen, Denmark. She walked alone through King's Square and down to the harbor, where a large steamer was docked. Wearing a thin dress and a black jacket, Valborg carried a canary in a bird cage in one hand and a wicker basket packed with her belongings in the other. She walked to the ship, climbed the long, narrow gangplank to the upper deck, then turned back to see a group of her schoolmates bidding her good-bye, waving small white handkerchiefs.

While holding on to the ship's railing, Valborg suddenly saw "a sweet, tear-stained face come into view." It was her mother. Unable to remain at home while her young daughter began this dramatic and courageous adventure, Henriette Rasmussen had rushed down to the harbor for one last glimpse of Valborg. Seeing her mother, Valborg whispered a prayer, "Oh God, be with us that we may meet again in that land out West."

Ahead of young Valborg was the great unknown. After a brief stopover in Liverpool, England, she would spend two weeks crossing the Atlantic Ocean aboard the *Wyoming* and six days on a train that would take her to Brigham City, Utah. There, she would work for three years on a dairy farm to pay off her immigration expenses. All these experiences came without the comfort and companionship of family members. Valborg's courage stemmed from her testimony of the restored gospel of Jesus Christ, which had been brought to her in Denmark by Willard Snow Hansen, a missionary for The Church of Jesus Christ of Latter-day Saints. With her baptism into the Church came a burning desire to join the Saints in "Zion." So Valborg left her family and playmates in Denmark, believing it was the will of the Lord.

This young Danish girl's experience, although daring and filled with enormous challenges, was not unique. Between 1840 and 1890, about forty thousand converts to Mormonism under the age of twenty-one crossed the oceans to gather with other Latter-day Saints in the Utah Territory. To read of their experiences is to come face to face with the courage and faith of some of the Mountain West's most tenacious pioneers. We can learn much from the vivid descriptions left by these young people.

A surprising number of young pioneers sailed to America without their parents. Many newly converted families were unable to afford to travel together. Some parents had no choice but to send their children on ahead with trusted neighbors or with Mormon missionaries. Other parents sailed to America ahead of their children, preparing the way for them to come later. Thus families often crossed the ocean one or two at a time until (hopefully) they were all together again in the Great Basin Kingdom of the American West.

Family separations were difficult for everyone. Augusta Dorius (Stevens), who emigrated in 1852 at the age of fourteen, first imagined that traveling to America with the family of a sea captain would be "a fine plan." But when the day of departure arrived, she had second thoughts:

"When I said farewell to my parents and brothers and sisters, and the steamboat sail[ed] out and my folks begin to fade out of sight, I felt alone and I surely felt badly. [I] wept as I then realized for the first time that I was alone to face the world, and that, too, on foreign soil. If I had known or realized how far that journey would be, I certainly would have felt worse."

Thomas Steed, age eighteen, had rarely been very far from his parents. He boarded the ship *Fanny* at Liverpool in 1844 with a heavy heart, leaving his family in England. His mother gave him a small Bible as a farewell gift. Inside

Long lines at port

she had inscribed: "Oh Tom, how can I let you go?" This Bible was a treasured keepsake for him the rest of his life.

Some young Latter-day Saints emigrated against the wishes of one or both parents. Charles Symons, who was eighteen when he emigrated in 1864, boarded the sailing vessel *Hudson* without his father's permission. He wrote:

"My father and Mr. Pardoe (to whom I was apprenticed) heard the news of our leaving for Utah and came to prevent us, following us down the Thames [River] and the English Channel in a tug[boat]. But we had too big a start, so they gave up the chase."

Emily Hodgetts (Lowder)'s departure for America was even more dramatic. She writes of the scene that occurred when she boarded the *Enoch Train* with her mother and sister:

"When father received the news [that we were leaving], he hastened to Liverpool with officers. He followed us [in a boat], and we were still in the Irish Channel and not yet on the open sea. Father paid the captain of [our] vessel one hundred sovereigns to cast anchor for one hour. We all hid. His time was about expired when mother finally gave herself up. He did not force mother to

A storm-tossed ship at sea

go back, but through kind persuasion, telling her that he would sell out and come to Utah [later], she went with him. I was fifteen, and my sister Marie, was seventeen. We came on alone to Boston." Emily's parents never did join her in America.

Once onboard, young ocean voyagers faced new trials. Nearly all emigrants suffered from seasickness. Emma Neat (Bennett) wrote that within thirty minutes of their ship's departure from Liverpool, she watched with alarm as her mother became desperately seasick. Her description of the ship's movement explains why people's stomachs were churning: "The ship's motion . . . was, first it would dip forward, then backward, then to the right, then to the left, then it would repeat those movements over again."

Fifteen-year-old Jensine Marie Jensen (Moulton) slept onboard the *Wyoming* in 1874 with only a small, wooden picket fence separating her head from three fat steers also making the journey. She wrote: "I was so deathly sick, laying there on the bare floor vomiting, and almost straining my life out. I couldn't raise my head, not a pillow or a mat under me. I was too sick to care or even think about [it.]"

Johanna Kirstine Larsen (Winters) was among a group of Latter-day Saints on the *Manhattan*. These emigrants shared their voyage with two hundred cows being shipped from Denmark to England. The North Sea was particularly rough during their journey. Johanna sympathized greatly with the cows, who "were just as sick as we were." If seasickness is bad for humans, who have one stomach, think how bad it is for cows, who have four stomachs!

Although most young people suffered from seasickness, nearly everyone fully recovered during the voyage, or at least upon their arrival in America. However, deaths at sea caused by dehydration and a variety of diseases were not uncommon, particularly among the oldest and youngest travelers. Most personal accounts mention the sobering experience of watching fellow travelers being buried at sea. Margaret Robertson (Salmon), age ten, witnessed the death and burial of her sister. "One of the thirty-eight who died while at sea was my bright-eyed sister Elizabeth, three years old," she wrote. "I can never forget the look of agony on my mother's face when her little girl's body was put overboard, one of four that day."

Sarah Davis (Carter) lost her two brothers, Rhuben and Levi, to an outbreak of smallpox on their ship, the *Windermere,* in 1854. "It almost killed my mother," she wrote, "to see those two darlings, with weights attached to their feet, slide into those shark-infested waters."

Mary M. Fretwell (Davis) describes in more detail the burial procedure that became all too familiar to young pioneers crossing the ocean in the nineteenth-century:

"There was one death on board—a child, and it seemed a sad sight to see it buried at sea. They dress the baby and then sew it up in sacking, then lay it on a board and put one end on the railing of the ship. Then, [they] have prayers and services, and then upend the board and the body slides into the sea."

In addition to the agony of sickness and disease aboard ship, most young travelers endured the terror of at least one storm at sea. As their ship was tossed like a barrel on the heaving, angry water, terrified passengers turned to their only hope for safety—their Heavenly Father. William Henry Bradfield, who was six years old when he crossed the Atlantic Ocean in 1868, describes his six-week experience aboard the *John Bright:*

"Nearly all the time the sea was wild and stormy. One night Captain McGaw told the Saints . . . if they believed there was a God, they had better ask for help. We children were clinging to mother's dress and crying. If ever there were prayers offered up, it was that night, and they were answered! [The] next day was a beautiful day and we children went on deck where we could see the rigging all torn away and the masts cracked."

Annie Batt (Bird Caffall), who was four years old in 1868, remembered that she and her sister were lashed to the mast of the *John Bright* during a particularly violent storm to keep their bodies from being washed overboard. Mary C. Simmons, age five, was laced to her sleeping berth on the *Hudson* for most of the trip to keep her from falling out when the voyage became rough.

In addition to the terrible storms they weathered, captains of sailing vessels and steamers alike had to show caution to avoid collisions with icebergs and other ships. Mary Ann Chappell (Warner), aboard the *John Bright* at age six, wrote of their ship's collision with another:

"One day when the air was dense with fog, another ship rammed into us [causing] a jagged hole in the side of our ship which immediately began to fill with water. All hands were called to man the pumps. The sailors dumped all excess baggage overboard, including my mother's prized feather beds, with the exception of one which she refused to part with, saying if it went down she would go with it. Clothing was taken and supposedly dumped overboard, but later my father discovered a sailor wearing some of his clothing."

Considering the dangers facing these relatively small ships as they crossed the oceans, it is a remarkable thing to note that between 1840 and 1890, not a single vessel carrying Mormon emigrants across the Atlantic Ocean was lost at sea—not one went down. This is in sharp contrast to the fact that at least fifty-nine non-Latter-day Saint immigrant ships were lost at sea while crossing the Atlantic just between the years of 1847–1853, alone. However, on the Pacific Ocean, the *Julia Ann* was wrecked in 1855 while bound from Sydney, Australia, to San Francisco. Twenty-eight of her fifty-six passengers were Mormons. Only five Latter-day Saints drowned in that accident; the others were miraculously saved.

The success rate of the Latter-day Saints can be attributed to divine intervention. Chartered vessels which carried Mormons across the Atlantic Ocean were carefully selected and prayers of safety were offered before emigrants left the docks of Liverpool, England. Furthermore, the power of the priesthood was called on at times of dangerous storms at sea. As a result, Mormon passengers placed great confidence and faith in their ability to arrive safely in America. Mary Ann Rawlings (Aveson), who emigrated at age twelve aboard the *Hudson*, wrote:

"The boat rolled and tossed and, of course, we had a storm at sea. Indeed, what would a sea voyage be without one? The steerage passengers were all locked down and told to be comfortable and everything would be all right. We had no fear. We were Mormons and we said, 'No ship would go down with such a precious cargo!'"

The success rate of Latter-day Saint voyages was also well known among non-Mormon sea captains, and most of them appreciated and admired their Mormon "cargo." For example, in 1872, onboard the *Minnesota,* Captain J. Morgan comforted a frightened eleven-year-old Latter-day Saint girl and other passengers at the time of a raging storm. Mary Ellison (Vincent) wrote: "During the worst of the storm, the dear old captain told us to be of good cheer for he always felt assured he would be safe if he had Mormon emigrants on board."

When they weren't holding on for dear life during a violent storm, or tossing and turning from the nauseating discomfort of seasickness, pioneer girls and boys found plenty to do aboard the ships to pass the time. Written accounts

Six companies of Saints (totaling 1,308) crossed the Atlantic on this single-screw steamship called the Manhattan.

are filled with memories of Mormon youngsters playing checkers and tag, singing, dancing, and enjoying their front-row view of interesting marine life. Ebenezer Farnes, age nineteen, enjoyed watching a porpoise "as fat as a pig" playing in the water next to their ship, the *William Tapscott.* Youngsters thrilled to see spouting whales, flying fish, and sharks. One girl even thought she saw a mermaid! Mary Ann Stucki (Hafen), who was six years old at the time of her voyage aboard the *Underwriter,* remembered with a smile:

"One afternoon while we were playing on the deck, one of the sailors pointed out a mermaid. I looked but could see only what seemed to be a lady's head above the water. The sailors told how mermaids would come up to comb their hair and look into a mirror. They said it was a sure sign of storm. Sure enough there arose a great storm next day."

Friendships were frequently struck up between the Mormon children and the often-crusty sailors. Youngsters enjoyed watching the sailors scrub the deck, sing, climb the rigging, and haul fish aboard for food. Even the captains occasionally agreed to participate in a rousing game of jump rope or marbles. With patience and a little creativity, most of these young pioneers found ways to enjoy the voyage.

The close of the first part of the journey was announced by the long-anticipated shout of "Land ahoy!" Seeing land in the distance signaled the end of one great adventure and the beginning of another—the overland journey to Nauvoo, 1840–1846, and later to the Rocky Mountains, beginning in 1847.

For those who had family waiting for them in the Utah Territory, images of a happy reunion must have occupied their thoughts. For those traveling ahead of their parents or with their parents, questions about their future remained: What does the Salt Lake Valley look like? Where will we live? What kind of work will we find? Will we get to meet the prophet?

These questions would be answered soon enough. For now, as they stepped ashore in New York City, Boston, Philadelphia, or New Orleans, it was time for excitement, gratitude, and relief. Mary Ann Stucki (Hafen) describes her company's reaction upon their arrival in America:

"At last we saw the lights of New York City. How the people did shout and toss their hats in the air for joy! I remember best my first meal on shore, because we were served with good light bread and sweet milk. After long weeks of zwieback, or hard tack, and dried pea soup, this was a happy change."

Other changes were ahead for the immigrants as they stepped ashore onto American soil. Some changes would be wonderful; others would bring enormous challenges, testing their souls to the limit.

It is exciting to read the personal writings of these intrepid young pioneers. They contributed as profoundly as their parents and leaders to the building of the Lord's kingdom in the latter days. We invite you to enjoy and to learn from these stories of courage, terror, joy, loneliness, mischief, faith, prayer, and divine guidance.

Folmer, Arnie, and Paul Jorgensen

PART ONE

Leaving the Homeland

"He that loveth father or mother more than me is not worthy of
me: and he that loveth son or daughter more than me is not worthy of me.
And he that taketh not his cross, and followeth
after me, is not worthy of me."
—Matthew 10:37–38

For many young emigrants, the thought of boarding a tall, strong-looking sailing ship and traveling deep into the great unknown sounded like a grand and exciting adventure. The hard part came when it was time to say good-bye to loved ones who would remain behind.

As Mormon missionaries converted thousands to the faith, many families were divided over religious beliefs. Sometimes a father joined the Church, but his wife refused baptism. Sometimes the mother and children were converted, but the father did not believe the gospel message. So, as converts set sail for America, many families experienced tearful farewells. Young people said good-bye to the people they would probably never see again: treasured friends, dearly loved grandparents, aunts, uncles, and cousins.

Children crossing the ocean also said good-bye to familiar surroundings—streams where they loved to fish, sledding hills, the corner bakery, beloved orchards, and school yards filled with their chums. Everything would be different in the New World. After arriving in America, many pioneer children had to learn a new language, get used to a new climate, and eat foods they had never seen before. As they arrived in New York Harbor, they saw new clothes, heard new dialects, and were exposed to new diseases.

Most young Mormon travelers fared very well, often adjusting better than their parents. Before long, Zion became their home. Very few ever regretted their decision to gather with the Saints in the West.

Many families experienced tearful farewells.

James Thomas Sutton holding a child

James Thomas Sutton

"We would not have turned back had we been given the chance."

BORN: October 2, 1848, Stratford, England
PARENTS: Henry William and Elizabeth Ford Sutton
SAILING DATE: June 3, 1864
SHIP: *Hudson*
AGE: 15

In 1864 . . . my parents decided to come to Utah for the sake of their religion. We were all anxious to go but we met with a lot of opposition from all those who knew us. Mr. Wean [my father's employer] tried to dissuade father by saying, "Henry, if you will change your mind, I'll give you a better job and I'll send your three boys to school. They can learn all it is possible for them to learn and then I'll apprentice them to any trade they want to follow. It won't cost you a penny."

In spite of this my father adhered to his original decision, and in the summer of that year we joined an emigration train and left London docks on the sailing vessel, *Hudson*, June 1, 1864. There were [863] Saints on board. That

11

The Hudson *completed two successful voyages bringing Latter-day Saint immigrants
to America, the first in 1864 and the second in 1867.*

was a sight to be remembered! Some were crying, some were laughing and others fainting at the thoughts of leaving their loved ones never to see them again. My father fainted on the deck as the ship began pulling away from the wharf. We thought for a few minutes that my brother Henry would not be with us. My cousin, James Thomas, was holding him on the dock trying to keep him from leaving but at the last moment he broke away and with a run and a big jump, caught hold of one of the ropes on the side of the boat and climbed aboard.

Captain Pratt, a cousin to Parley P. Pratt, was our captain. A fine man, and a good sailor. He piloted our ship to Castle Garden, New York, safe in the harbour after battling head winds all the way across. There were 1025 people all told on board ship. We stood the trip fairly well. The fare was coarse but substantial. Hard ship's biscuits, fat beef, pork, beans and rice were our chief foods. Mother brought a small coop of chickens, two hens and a rooster, across with her. The few eggs we gathered were surely enjoyed.

Mother was very sick on the ship and could not eat anything until we got an egg and made it into a custard. She was able to eat that and so gained strength. We had a few deaths aboard. When that happened the body was wrapped in a sheet, weighted, and laid on a plank. It was then taken to the side of the ship, the plank tipped, and the body slid off into the ocean. "The billows rolled as they rolled before . . . many a prayer did hallow the wave as they sank beneath in a traveler's grave."

At that time the Civil War was going on and as we neared our destination, the [Confederate] warship, *Alabama,* pulled alongside our ship to determine what kind of freight was aboard. The [*Alabama's*] sailors cried out to us to "say your prayers, you Mormons, you are all going down!" But we were spared. We were all immigrants from other countries and they dared not sink us.

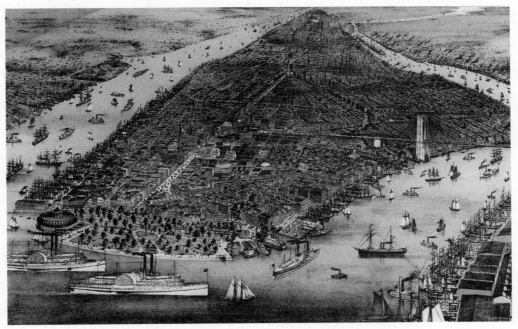

Castle Garden, New York, is the circular building in the lower left corner.

It took us seven and one-half weeks to make the trip across and at the end our ship was piloted into [New York] harbor. All our luggage was taken to the custom house and examined. We were all passed on by doctors. As the doctor finished with us boys he turned to mother and said heartily, "your three boys are all alright!" If there had been any suspicion by the doctor that we were not as we should be in regard to health, we would have been kept in quarantine.

After we were through there, we were all loaded on a steamboat and taken up the [Hudson] river for a distance. Finally we were unloaded from [the steamboat] and eventually found ourselves on a train ready for our overland

European immigrants disembark at Castle Garden.

I well remember leaving England. We went to the train with my oldest brother Joe, who had to remain in England two years to finish his apprenticeship as a shoemaker. We all felt very badly about leaving him. I remember how mother cried. We sailed on the ship *Arkwright* leaving Liverpool May 30th, 1866.

—*Ellen Burton Beazer emigrated at age 7, in 1866, aboard the* Arkwright.

journey westward. The cars were without decent accommodations. We had to sit on our luggage for seats. People were riding in cattle cars or any kind they could get. It was desperately hard on those who were sick and on the older people.

Now we reached the [Civil] war zone.* We saw quite a bit of action by the soldiers and by the Indians. Many times we saw smoke signals from the tops of the mountains. One of the railroad bridges was destroyed and we had to unload all the luggage, take it down through the creek, up the other side and into some cattle cars that were handy there—dirty or clean, it made no difference. The next station we came to was burned to the ground. The train was fired at by soldiers and one of the cars was afire as a result. Often at night officers came through the train

* *Note: This was not until the Saints reached the state of Missouri.*

searching for deserters. At times the engine and tender were alive with soldiers shooting at rebels tearing up track. Of course fear and horror were experienced by all of us but we would not have turned back had we been given the chance.

We finally reached the end of the railroad tracks and had to prepare ourselves for the journey across the Plains. We stayed about two weeks getting ready for the westward march. The provisions had to be divided and all arrangements made.

We were between three and four months coming across the Plains and one weary day we found ourselves traveling down Weber Canyon within one day's travel of our destination—Salt Lake City. Captain Hyde had gone on ahead when Bishop Cannon from Salt Lake met us. It was in October and there was snow on the ground. We had all gone through a great deal of suffering and were very happy to pull into the 8th Ward Square, the immigrant's camping grounds. The [Salt Lake] City and County Building now stands on that spot.

James Thomas Sutton eventually married Linda Burch in the Endowment House in Salt Lake City. They lived in Grantsville, Utah, and had three children. After Linda's death, James married Annie Cooke in the Logan Temple. She and James had eleven children. James raised sheep, operated a store, and owned real estate in Grantsville. He died January 6, 1940, at the age of ninety-one.

SOURCE: Sutton, James T. Autobiography. In Our Pioneer Heritage, *compiled by Kate B. Carter, 17:296–99. 20 vols. Salt Lake City: Daughters of Utah Pioneers, 1974.*

Margaret Miller Watson (DeWitt)

"Haven't you any folks to look after you?"

BORN: January 10, 1841, in Annahill, Lanarkshire, Scotland
PARENTS: John and Jane Josea Miller Watson
SAILING DATE: June 21, 1857
SHIP: *Isaac Wright*
AGE: 16

I was born in Glasgow, Scotland, January 16, 1841; the youngest of a family of nine children. . . . Among my earliest recollections of my father, who died when I was a small child, is my seeing him wrapped in quilts seated in a chair, while I played peek-a-boo with him through the glass in our door.

When I was about fifteen years of age my sister Jane, six years older than I, joined the Mormon Church and emigrated to America. The members of the family felt that by so doing she had brought great disgrace to our family.

My mother died when I was twelve years old, and I lived with an elder sister, Belle, who sold [our parents' home] and rented one little room for the two of us. During this time my sister Jane wrote to me in care of a friend, Agnes McKay, urging me to attend the Mormon meetings and investigate their religion for myself.

This I did secretly—going to the meetings when my sister supposed I was attending night school. I was able to attend several meetings conducted by the Mormon elders before my sister discovered my deception, which she finally learned from the factory girls. Thinking she was doing the proper thing, she gave me a severe whipping and warned me not to go near the elders again. However, this only served to strengthen my determination to find out for myself all about the Mormons and Mormonism.

I still continued my secret correspondence with my sister Jane, who lived in Holyoke, Massachusetts; and she sent me money to pay my passage across the ocean. I remember going to the bank and getting the money which I concealed in the bosom of my dress in the day-time and in my shoe at night. Very soon after this I left my sister Belle's home. We had eaten breakfast, and I left as if I were on my way to the factory. I saw the clothes spread on the green to bleach (she had washed the day before) and I picked up my night-cap and slipped it into my pocket. This was all I took with me except the clothes I stood up in.

I went directly to my friends, the McKays, who informed me that the next sailboat would not leave for two weeks. I couldn't go back home to Belle, so my kind Mormon friends, the McKays, hid me up for two weeks in the home of a widow who boarded me: the McKays paid her for her trouble. During this time the McKays outfitted me with clothes for my journey.

Scandinavian girl just before her voyage to America

Bills had been posted and rewards offered for my capture, so, fearing detection, I disguised myself when I went to the sailboat. Just before boarding the ship I posted a letter to my sister Belle telling her not to continue her search for me as I was on my way to America. I crossed the gang-plank and entered the ship. Then I went below into the steerage until the ship had started.

I then went up on deck and took a last fond farewell of my native land. I was overcome with conflicting emotions as I saw it disappearing from my sight. For, though I was glad and eager to come to America, where I could learn more about Mormonism and join my sister Jane, yet I felt sad to leave forever my

It was a very interesting sight to witness the coming together of 900 Latter-day Saints, consisting of English, Scotch, Welsh, Germans, Hollanders, Swiss, Scandinavian, Danish, and a very few French. At the fore end of the ship, apartments and berths were arranged for 200 consisting of mostly Irish emigrants to the United States. . . .

Our people were very busy locating themselves in their berths by day, fastening their trunks and belongings to the deck so that all would be firm and not be disturbed by the ship's motion when at sea. At dusk, groups would gather and visit with each other, singing the songs of Zion and relating incidents that had occurred in getting to the big boat, and also of their history since becoming members of the Church. But oh! what a happy crowd, all bent on doing the will of the Lord and keeping his commandments.

—*Charles William Symons emigrated at age 18, in 1864, aboard the* Hudson.

native land, my brothers and sisters and friends. I extended my arms and cried, "Good-bye forever, old home." The ship, the *Isaac Wright*, bore me off.

Soon after leaving I became violently seasick and lay on the bare deck for relief. Having taken nothing with me except my clothing, I had nothing to lie on. A young woman came near me, saying, "How's this? Haven't you any folks to look after you? But no, I mustn't talk; I must *do* something."

She went to the cook-room and made a little tea and toast. As I partook of it, my stomach became settled, so that I could get up and around. Soon I became more adjusted to life on board ship. From Liverpool to New York, we were on the sailing vessel six weeks and three days.

When we landed at New York the McKay girl's folks met us there. A large crowd was present as we were getting off the ship. I kept saying aloud, "O have you seen my sister?" I hadn't heard the popular song then being sung, entitled, "O Have You Seen My Sister?" At once someone in that great throng caught up the words and sang it while the whole merry crowd began singing and laughing.

Young boys like Johan Johansen, of Norway, often had their pictures taken in pint-sized sailor suits.

I took the train from New York to Springfield, Massachusetts, where my sister met me. Words cannot express the joy of our meeting. I went with her to her home in Holyoke. There I remained with her and a group of emigrant girls. We worked in a factory, earning the money to pay our way to Utah. Having had experience in working in the factories in Glasgow, [Scotland] where there were five hundred steam looms on one floor, I felt at home in the work. They started me out with two looms; when my sister saw that I could handle them easily and still have plenty of spare time, she said to the manager, "My sister is an ambitious little girl and I'm sure she can handle more looms when you can give them to her."

They gave me four for awhile, but soon increased it to six, the most ever given to any experienced girls in the factory.

I made it a point always to be prompt; and the watchman would laugh as he held his lantern so that he could see my face as I sat at the big doors each morning waiting for him to open them and let me in. The minute the engine started I was at my loom. Some of the girls were always ten minutes or more late; when they remarked at my higher wages on pay-day, it was pointed out to them that ten minutes each day will soon amount to dollars and cents.

We received our pay in an office adjoining the factory. Here two men counted out the money, which was held in a big, seamless sack. The books were opened and the numbers of the looms were given. Then the girls were paid in cash. [When] I received my wages, I often heard the men whisper one to another, "Is that the one?" I was small for my age and my skill as a factory hand was talked about among the workers.

We worked in this factory for about three

About the year 1854, my parents joined The Church of Jesus Christ of Latter-day Saints, which, as might be expected, brought down upon their heads the ridicule and scorn of their very religious parents, and [they] were looked upon as being a disgrace to their families.

At that time my father was engaged in the mercantile business for a livelihood and had been very successful, but as soon as it became known that he had joined that hated and despised people known as the Mormons, a great change was soon apparent. His old patrons withdrew their patronage and did all they could to injure his business. As a result, he closed down at a great loss, which left him very much reduced in circumstances.

In the spring of 1856, we emigrated to America.

—*Ebenezer Crouch emigrated at age 5, in 1856, aboard the* Horizon.

years. Our boarding house was managed by two old maid sisters who had rented a large house especially for factory girls. We paid them each month; and outside of our board, lodging, and clothes, we saved every cent for our journey across the Plains.

My sister [Jane] left for Utah three weeks before I did, as there was not room for both of us in the first company. I handed to the president of the branch sixty dollars in cash to pay my way to Utah.

Before leaving for Zion, however, I had been baptized and confirmed a member of the Church. My sister and I had attended regularly the LDS services in Holyoke. Each meeting strengthened my faith, though I had believed the Gospel to be true from the first time I heard the Elders preach it in Glasgow. On account of the bitter opposition manifest by anti-Mormons there, my baptism was performed at night. When I was taken to the river the ice was broken, and there I was baptized.

I traveled across the Plains with Thomas Lyons, his invalid wife, and five children. They had two hired teamsters, each driving a large wagon-load of goods. I took care of their five children and cooked every bite that was eaten by our outfit of ten, from the time we left Florence, Nebraska, until we reached

Advertising poster for the ship Emerald Isle. *This vessel brought three companies of Saints across the Atlantic.*

Salt Lake City. I walked all the way across the Plains, carrying the baby much of the time. Sister Lyons had to be lifted in and out of the wagon, and had a special chair to sit on. . . .

We were three months crossing the Plains, under [Captain] Edward Stevenson. My sister heard of the [approach of our] company through the "Pony Express" and was ready to meet me. She had arranged for [me] a place to work— for a Sister Elizabeth Howard, who lived eight miles south of Salt Lake City at Big Cottonwood. My sister had a place in Salt Lake [City] and we often visited.

Margaret married Abel Alexander DeWitt on March 15, 1860. Abel joined the Church two weeks later. They had six children while living in Big Cottonwood. Brigham Young called them to move to Kanab, Utah, where they had three more children. They moved again, this time to Springerville, Arizona, where three more children were born, making a total of twelve. They then moved to nearby Woodruff, Arizona. Margaret was known by her friends as "a loving, laughing, witty little Scottish lady." She loved to read and especially enjoyed attending Relief Society. Margaret had a saying: "Thank God every morning when you get up, that you have something to do which must be done, whether you like it or not. Being forced to work and forced to do your best will breed in you temperance, self-control, diligence, and strength of will." Margaret died on February 28, 1930, in Woodruff, Arizona.

SOURCE: DeWitt, Margaret Watson. "Autobiography of Margaret Miller Watson DeWitt." Relief Society Magazine 16.7 (July 1929): 379–83.

John Allen Sutton, Sr.; his son Richard S.; Richard's son, Dr. Richard J.; and the doctor's son Dell

John Allen Sutton

"No tongue could describe the scene between those decks."

BORN: November 16, 1834, Leire, Leicestershire, England
PARENTS: John and Ann Allen Sutton
SAILING DATE: March 12, 1854
SHIP: *John M. Wood*
AGE: 19

When I was fifteen years old] there came to our village two men professing to be Mormons, or Latter-day Saints, by name, Edward Stevenson and Henry Bowns. They held their meetings in the open air and many people flocked to hear them. I, with others, was very much taken up with their teachings as they were feasible and seemed according to scripture.

For several weeks these men came Sunday after Sunday. I still investigated their principles, but being young I was too timid to talk to them concerning their doctrine. . . . Not until November eleventh, of the same year, 1849, did I make up my mind to ask them to baptize me, as I was thoroughly convinced that the doctrine was true and according to scriptures. I then spoke to one of the elders, Henry Sanders, who told me if I believed, I could be baptized. I replied that I did.

This was on Sunday. There was a great commotion in the place. There were many enemies to this people already in the village who declared that if the [Elder] went to baptize me, they would drown him. Not being daunted, we started to the stream of water and I believe nearly one hundred people followed us. The Elder told the people that he was going to perform one of the ordinances of the gospel of Jesus Christ and if they would be quiet, he would show them how it was done. He then took me into the waters and baptized me, and not a word was said by any person. Thus I entered into a new life to me.

After receiving confirmation on the next Sabbath Day, I became very fervent in the performance of all the duties they required of me. My father and mother, brothers and sisters thought I was very foolish and that it would not last long, but finding that not to be the case and that many people were joining the Church in the little village, persecution began to rage and my greatest enemies were those of my own household.

I had now made up my mind to leave the land of my nativity and go to America, to Salt Lake City, it being a part of our religion to gather from the world. So strong was this feeling on me to gather, that nothing seemed to stay the progress. Still I was poor.

Three months prior to my starting to America, I had no means, but President John Angus told me if I wished to go that the way

The letter came from Liverpool telling us passages for all our family had been secured on the sailing ship *John J. Boyd* and telling us to sell everything we would not need on the journey and come to Liverpool in site of three days to get on board the ship which would sail April 22, 1862. This letter caused great rejoicing. Brother Sam ran around the house shouting, "Boys this is the best letter [that] ever came to our home."
—*William Lindsay emigrated at age 12, in 1862, aboard the* John J. Boyd.

I can remember when [my parents] received the telegram telling them to be in Liverpool at twelve o'clock that night ready to sail for America. They packed just our clothing and what could be put in a trunk and had to leave everything else.

I had a half-sister who was staying with some people in London at the time and my parents sent them a telegram telling them to put her on the train so she would meet us in Liverpool ready to sail with us. She was either put on the wrong train or something but when we reached Liverpool she was no where to be found.

Mother and father were both worried and kept walking up and down the platform. It was just a few minutes of sailing time when they finally found her and she was crying and so frightened and had lost her baggage. She had nothing but the clothing she was wearing until we reached America and mother could buy her some more.

—*Emma Palmer Manfull emigrated at age 8, in 1874, aboard the* Idaho.

would be opened for me. I placed such confidence in his word that I commenced to make preparations to leave.

The fare from Liverpool to Salt Lake City was ten pounds in what was known as "The Ten Pound Company." It appeared impossible for me to raise that amount, but by saving all the money I could get hold of I managed to get enough to pay my fare to New Orleans.

An incident occurred at this time that seems fraught with danger to my taking departure. In consequence of my not being of age, my father said he would stop me from going.

After all preparations were made, my fare across the ocean paid, and my boxes and things sent to Liverpool, I went to bid my folks goodbye and my father was away from home. I feared he had gone to get an officer to stop me but I said farewells and started out without seeing my father and went to the house of one John Douglas in the same village and stayed for a few hours. In the meantime my father came home and made inquiries for me. They told him I was gone. He said, "Go and bring him back, I want to see him before he goes." So my brother, Thomas, came down to the house where they supposed I would be and asked for me. I questioned my brother as to whether there was an officer waiting for me and he said there was not, but that my father wished to see me before I made my departure.

I went home and my father said to me, "Then you are determined to go, are you?" I said, "Yes, father, that is my intention." He said, "I think you are very foolish, you do not know where you are going, you are going to a new country and you have no money, nor friends. Now if you will stay with us for one year I will give you this (throwing his purse on the table) besides paying you good wages, and will send you off comfortable." I told him I would not stay if he gave me all he possessed. Then he said he would not give me a farthing. I shook hands with him and bid him farewell. He then called me back and gave me a sovereign, which proved a great help to me at Liverpool.

I took the train and arrived at Liverpool with many others going to cross the ocean on the same ship. In consequence of the ship not being fitted up properly, we were detained in Liverpool two weeks, from the first to the twelfth of March, and the expense incurred used up all my money with the exception of four shillings. On the twelfth day of March we went on board the ship, *John M. Wood,* with six or seven hundred passengers, all members of The Church of Jesus Christ of Latter-day Saints. The company was presided over by Robert Campbell.

Scandinavian boys after their arrival in Utah

After setting sail on the Irish Channel we encountered a terrific storm. The captain ordered all the hatchways down and kept all the passengers in the lower deck. No tongue could describe the scene between those decks for 48 hours. Boxes pitching, pots and everything loose flying about, and nearly all the ship's company seasick. Such an experience I shall never forget while on earth.

On the second day at noon we were driven back within sight of Liverpool. After this we set sail and got onto the Atlantic Ocean. Nothing of interest occurred, having fair weather until we passed the Island of Cuba, when a terrific storm came along which tore the sails to shreds and moved the main mast nearly six inches out of its socket. But it was all over in fifteen minutes.

We soon arrived at the Gulf of Mexico, where we were becalmed for about ten days, the sea being smooth as glass.

We finally came to within twenty miles of the city of New Orleans. After some trouble in negotiating with a steamtug to take us over the bar, we were towed into the mouth of the Mississippi River. Next day, after seven weeks of ocean voyage, we landed in New Orleans. There were two deaths and two births on the voyage.

Preparations were made as quickly as possible to take the company from New Orleans to St. Louis. How to go I did not know as all the money I had was four shillings. Finally President McDonald loaned me $2.50 which took me to St. Louis. The voyage up the river was fraught with many events. The cholera was very high and many of the passengers died. Some would be taken down with the disease and would die within three hours; but fortunately my health was good and I was able to assist in taking care of the sick and in burying the dead.

When we arrived within four miles of St. Louis, the captain feared he would be fined for carrying so many passengers, so he put four hundred of us off and we walked to St. Louis. I arrived in St. Louis with only five cents in my pocket, not knowing any person nor where I should go. Fortune favored me. Passing through the streets I met one of our ship's company who was very pleased to see me. He took me down to a restaurant and I ate a very pleasant meal and I thought I had never had better food before and never expected to again, so hungry was I.

My next trouble was to know how to get up to the frontier, a town [called Westport, Missouri], the outfitting post for the emigration that year. After resting overnight with my friend, I traveled around St. Louis to try to find work at my trade. All the shops seemed full and I could not get work till I came across the "Espenshied Wagon Company" where they told me to come to work in the morning. I started to go to work and got near the shop. Still, something told me not to go in, for what reason I could not tell. I stood for a few minutes and then started down to the wharf. I went on board the Thursday Packet, *F. X. Aubry,* and inquired if they wanted any hands to work up the river. They said they did, so I hired to them to go to Council Bluffs for a dollar a day and my board. I being somewhat green as to the work on boats, I suffered many insults and much abuse, for the mate was a very cruel man, especially to new hands.

While on the boat, the engineer found out I was a blacksmith, so he wanted me to work in the shop, which pleased me very much; but the mate swore I should not work there and that I should stand my regular watch, so fearing more cruelty from the hands of the mate, the engineer locked me in the iron grated shop. When my watch came around the mate went to hunt me up at my

When weather permitted, passengers spent much of their time on deck.

berth, and with oaths, swore he would kill me if I did not come out and go on my watch. I made no answer. He then took a piece of timber and broke my berth down, but not finding me he went to the engineer, who told him that I could not go on my watch as I was working for him. An altercation then took place which nearly resulted in the death of one of them.

Finally the boat arrived at Kansas City, which city at that time comprised one store and two homes. I informed the mate that I wished now to leave the boat and asked him for my pay. Finally after a volley of oaths they paid me my six dollars and let me go. I had now enough money to pay what I had borrowed and a nice margin to spare, the sum of three dollars.

We waited at Kansas City some time, the cholera being very bad, and spent our time in preparing wagons, making ox shoes, ox yokes and bows, and fitting up.

One day upon going into the store at Kansas City I saw a coin on the floor. I looked at it and placed my foot upon it. Finally I picked it up and found it to be a sovereign. Knowing it did not belong to me I went to camp and told John Angus what I had found and asked him what I should do with it. "Well, my

The travelers' chaos

boy," he said, "If anyone inquires for the lost money, give it to him; if not, I don't know of anyone who needs it worse than you do and I shall consider it a Godsend to you."

My next trouble was to know how to go across the Plains, one thousand miles. I hadn't money to pay my fare and my case looked rather dark, as all the trains that hired men to drive teams had gone. I finally succeeded making a contract with a man by the name of Jarvis to take me across the Plains. I was to fix up his wagons and milk his cows on the journey. Therefore, in [mid-June, 1854] the company moved out on the Plains and was organized. There were about one hundred wagons and Job Smith was appointed captain. . . .

Arriving at Platte Bridge, it was thought best to divide the company into three parts. Here an incident occurred which seemed as though I was to be left on the Plains, for Mr. Jarvis' provisions had given out and he told me he could not take me any further. Still I had found a friend in Mr. Ford, now living in

Centerville, Utah. He had lost two of his sons who had died of cholera. Mr. Ford told me he would be glad if I would come and drive his team. . . . I drove Mr. Ford's team till he arrived at Salt Lake City, which was on the twenty-third day of September, and we had made our camp at Jordan Bridge.

John married Eliza Billingham in England just before sailing to America. They agreed that he would go on ahead to make arrangements for work and to establish a place for them to live. John worked as a blacksmith in Salt Lake City to earn money for Eliza to immigrate, which she and her relatives did in 1856. Eliza died while traveling with the John A. Hunt wagon train, which was caught in the early winter storms of 1856.

John then married Margaret Shepherd in 1858, and they became the parents of eleven children. They lived in Salt Lake City and later West Weber until President Brigham Young called them, along with one hundred other families, to settle Bear Lake Valley, Idaho. John married Sarah Woolley in 1887, and they became the parents of two children. John served a mission to England and was proud to have three of his sons also serve missions to England. Working as a blacksmith, he frequently used the forceps in his shop to pull teeth if someone came in with a toothache. John and his family frequently provided accommodations for Church general authorities when they visited the Bear Lake area from Salt Lake City. He served as president of the Eleventh Quorum of the Seventies and was later ordained a high priest. John died May 11, 1913, in the home he had built for his family.

SOURCE: *Sutton, John Allen. Autobiography, 1–7, 9. LDS Church Archives. See also "John Allen Sutton Family," by Wealthy Fackrell in* History of Bear Lake Pioneers, *Daughters of Utah Pioneers, compiled by Edith Parker Haddock and Dorothy Hardy Matthews. Salt Lake City: Utah Printing Company, 1968. An additional source is* Life History of John Allen Sutton and His Family, *compiled by Sylvia S. Sharp and Donna S. Kuhre. Privately printed in 1994.*

Mary Haskin Parker (Richards)

"I must bid an everlasting adieu to my native land."

BORN: September 8, 1823, Chaigley, Lancashire, England
PARENTS: John, Sr., and Ellen Heskin Parker
SHIP: *Alliance* (commercial ship)
SAILING DATE: December 23, 1840
AGE: 17

My father occupied a small farm near the foot of Mount Longridge [in England] in one of the most beautiful valleys that my eyes ever beheld. The mountain stream ran singing by the door, joined by the warbling notes of unnumbered birds whose melody in the spring & summer together with other adjoining beauties made my home appear delightful.

About the third of September [1840] my parents commenced to make preparations to go to America. On the 5th [they] took leave of the house where they had lived for forty two years, and their native country. My sister Alice and myself accompanied them to Preston and at nine o'clock bade them goodbye.

It was a very dark night. After we lost sight of them, sister Alice fainted and it was some time before we could bring her to. It was indeed a gloomy night to us both. . . . I was very sick all the night. The next morning I took the railway car to Longridge eight miles, then walked six miles [home]. Was very sick all the way. Reached home about five in the eve[ning]. After this I was sick four weeks with the typhus fever.

On the 7th of December [1840] my brother Rodger, and George Rhodas come to see me. The latter informed me that he together with Bro. Bleasdale's folks intended to sail for America on the 12th [of December]. He told me if I would go with them he would furnish me whatsoever means I might be lacking to carry me to Nauvoo. My brother and the brethren of the Church counseled me to go. So I took leave of my sister Isabella on the 8th [of December 1840].

About eight in the morning I traveled about four miles & came to Mellerbrook. Found my sister Ann and stayed with her two hours. Then after taking some refreshment, took leave of her and her dear family, who wept much at my departure. Traveled eight miles on foot and about five in the evening came to my sister Ellen's house. Found her with a [new] little daughter near

Leaving home

I have memories of the packing [for our journey]. Only the most cherished or most useful things were to go. I took on the fever of packing and packed big rocks in the barrels. Two of these barrels had to be repacked because of this. One time at the close of a day of packing my sisters searched for my shoe and after some time I, in great fear, told them it was packed in the bottom of a trunk.

—*Sarah Ann Horsley emigrated at age 7, in May of 1882, aboard the* Nevada.

3 weeks old, herself very sick and also her husband. Stayed & took care of them that night and til noon the next day.

Then went to see my brother Richard's folks about two miles east. Stayed with them till evening, then went to Chipping, three miles northwest, to see my brother Robert's folks, then bid the family good bye. Bro. R[obert] came with me about a mile. He not being a [Latter-day] Saint I gave him my testimony in regard to my faith in the work which I had embraced and desired him to join the Church and to gather with the Saints that one day ere long I might see his face again. I then bade him good bye & left him in tears with but little hope that I should ever see his face [once] more.

The next day I visited among my friends, and at evening, attended a prayer meeting at Brother John's house which had been called on account of my [going] away. There was a number of brethren & sisters who spoke & promised us their prayers for our welfare. We had a good meeting, at the latter part of which I sang a few verses which I had composed as a farewell song to my brothers & sisters.

Spent that night it being the last with Sister Alice. The next morning I traveled one mile and took leave of the spot that gave me birth. Called to see our nearest neighbor Mrs. Tayler, who came with me about a quarter of a mile and wept most bitterly to part with me.

Never shall I forget the feeling that shrilled through my bosom this day while parting with all my dear Brothers & Sisters and all my kindred who were near & dear to me by the ties of nature, especially my dear sick sister and her companion who needed my assistance, to travel to a distant port; and from there to venture upon the wide expanded ocean [beyond, from] which to wander in a strange land.

Hope at intervals would glimmer in my bosom. There [in America] dwell my dear parents. But what if God should please to take them to himself? E'er I be permitted to see them? I must bid an everlasting adieu to my native land and to that dear spot that gave me birth. 'Tis true I was going with a family who had promised to befriend me. But what if they should forget their covenant and leave me a stranger in a strange land? The trial of parting with my friends together with these reflections caused me to give vent to my tears, which until this time I had endeavored to conceal.

Mary traveled to Liverpool, and from there she was to sail to America. Upon her arrival in Liverpool, however, she was informed that the man who had promised to pay her passage and expenses from New York to Nauvoo had been robbed of all his money.

Now our hopes were plighted. Sister Bleasdale says "Mary, the ship will sail in the morning. What shall we do?" I replied, "Our passage is paid. Our provisions are on board. Let us go to [New York]. The Lord is just as able to sustain us there as he is if we should remain here. And so long as we walk uprightly before him we shall have no cause to fear, for he has promised that he will never forsake those who put their trust in him."

On the 23rd [December] about 10 o'clock we drew anchor and set sail. . . . It was with feelings

I was alone. It was a dreary winter day on which I went to Liverpool. The company with which I was to sail were all strangers to me. When I arrived at Liverpool and saw the ocean that would soon roll between me and all I loved, my heart almost failed me. But I had laid my idols all upon the altar. There was no turning back.

—*Priscilla Mogridge Staines emigrated at age 20, in 1843, aboard the* Fanny.

of no ordinary kind that I took a last look upon my native shore, which was now fast fading away in the distance, and launched out upon the broad Atlantic Ocean.

Mary became the wife of Samuel Whitney Richards on January 29, 1846, in the Nauvoo Temple. Samuel then served a mission to Great Britain for two years. Mary crossed Iowa and lived in Winter Quarters until his return in May of 1848. During those two years, she wrote six journals about her daily activities. No other journals are known to have been written by her. The following year the family traveled to Salt Lake City, Utah. Samuel went back to England to serve as mission president two times, leaving Mary to carry on alone. Mary had six children, two of whom died young. She died in childbirth with her sixth baby on June 3, 1860, at the age of thirty-six. Her unnamed son also died at this time and was buried with her, next to her two other babies.

SOURCE: Ward, Maurine Carr, ed., Winter Quarters: The 1846–1848 Life Writings of Mary Haskin Parker Richards, 53–55, 58–61. Logan: Utah State University Press, 1996. *Some spelling and grammar have been modernized from original source.*

Valborg Henrietta Louise Rasmussen (Wheelwright)

"I was determined to persuade Mother to let me go."

BORN: June 3, 1875, Copenhagen, Denmark
PARENTS: Wilhelm Gotfred Matinus and Henriette Louise
Wilhelmine Lever Rasmussen
SAILING DATE: September 1, 1888
SHIP: *Wyoming*
AGE: 13

Valborg's father died at sea when she was just three months old, leaving her mother a widow with four young children. The family moved frequently as their mother sought employment.

ow peculiar it was that at this time [during my childhood in Denmark], and in these circumstances, I should meet two young schoolmates who were Mormons. A few months had passed since

The sea is more calm and beautiful. The wind is in our favor and although I long to see my friends in Cambridge, I console myself with the thought of going to Zion, to the promised land. Oh! Glorious thought!

—Charlotte Jarrold Hyder Evans emigrated at age 17, in 1851, aboard the Olympus.

Mother had moved, so I was beginning to make friends at Hindagal, the school I was attending. Among those friends were Hilda and Oscar Winkler, who lived only a block from our home. They were attractive children, near my own age of twelve.

On Sundays Mother worked at the hospital. . . . After I finished my chores, I would be quite alone; so when Oscar and Hilda invited me to visit their Mormon Sunday School, I was happy to go.

The Latter-day Saints met at Krystalgade on the second floor of a little building inside a court yard. We walked through a portal to get to the yard inside. There were many steps to climb, but at the top was a hall full of children and young people.

After I heard that first [Sunday School] lesson I wanted to go again and again. Every Sunday I would hurry to complete my duties by ten o'clock so that I would be ready when my two friends called for me. My Sunday School teacher, Mrs. Thor Nielson, was a convert. I liked her, and we became good friends. Of course, I learned a lot from Oscar and Hilda. Mother was working, so I usually spent the whole day at their home, and we would talk about the morning's lessons. . . .

My ears and heart had been opened by the messages I had heard on Sundays in the humble hall at Krystalgade. The Mormon faith brought a whole new life to me, even as a child. The missionaries spoke from the Bible; that is what really converted me. I knew what the Bible said, and the Mormon elders proved the truth of the gospel from the Bible. I knew that everything Elder Hansen taught Mother and me was true.

That spring brought a beautiful Easter morning, and I, as usual, was on my way to Sunday School. I had finished my chores and had to run to get there by ten o'clock. I was singing all the way. After Sunday School I saw Elder Hansen, and out of the clear blue sky he asked me, "How would you like to go to Zion with me?" From all the events of the past weeks and all I had learned of the gospel, I felt this was a direct call from God to be gathered with his people. I knew the chance would never present itself again. It was not going to be easy, but I was determined to persuade Mother to let me go.

At spring conference President Teasdale came and spoke. His words were inspired. To me the Spirit bore a marked interpreted message. I was fully converted to every truth he spoke. I talked with the elders and was not a bit frightened when Elder Hansen baptized me in the waters of "Langelinge."

But I had a hard task ahead of me. I begged Mother every day and tried to make her see how important it was that I go to Utah. I would listen to no argument from her. . . . I'd make her come and kneel down with me each morning before she went to work.

I had really never had anything so important to pray about before as this object now in view. Oh, I had had my small everyday wishes, but never a need so great that it required more than just a few minutes of prayer. This was different. I constantly asked my Heavenly Father to help Mother see the truthfulness of the gospel. It was the truth. I knew it was. It was a gift from God.

My mother was not well and was taken on board the ship before the time of sailing, while the sailors were still disinfecting and renovating the ship. Here my brother Charles was born with only one woman on board the ship to attend my mother. When the captain and doctor came on board the ship and found that a baby had been born they were delighted and thought it would bring good luck to the company. They asked the privilege of naming him. So the captain named him Charles Thornton McNeil after the boat, *Thornton,* . . . and [the] Captain Charles Collins.

—Margaret McNeil Ballard emigrated at age 10, in 1856, aboard the Thornton.

I couldn't have been more convinced of anything in my life than I was of that. And God was calling me to Zion. I preached all summer to my mother, my schoolmates—anyone who would listen: "He who is not willing to leave father, mother, for my name's sake, is not worthy of me." This was the scripture I quoted to substantiate my point of view. So many children didn't have a chance to go, and I did. Somehow I knew that I would go and that Mother would know it was the right thing for me to do.

After six weeks of prayer and meeting and talks with Elder Hansen, Mother gave her consent. After that, all the King's men couldn't have stopped me from going. Our neighbors thought it was a shameful thing for a mother to allow her

The Wyoming, *a British steamer, carried more Latter-day Saints across the Atlantic Ocean than any other vessel—a total of 10,473.*

daughter to do. All the people who had not cared at all if we had no food to eat or clothes to wear now shook their heads in horror at the thought of my leaving with those awful Mormons. . . .

The whole family thought Mother had lost her mind. [My older brother] Karl and his wife, a fine girl from Dresden, came to Copenhagen when they heard I was going to Utah. Aunt Amalie came down from Middlefort. Both of them offered me homes with them if I would not go with Elder Hansen. They could not understand. Had I been looking for a better home I'm sure I would have enjoyed Germany or the Danish isles, but I was about my Father's business.

One day the police knocked on our door and served Mother with a summons. She and I went to the police court to be questioned. I was so frightened my heart stood still. Could they stop me from going? They tried. They asked us many questions and attempted to show that I was not my mother's child. No

Passengers getting settled in their berths.

one could believe that any mother would let her youngest child leave home on such an incredible journey. But there was nothing they could do once Mother gave indisputable proof that she had given birth to me. I'm sure it was my relatives who instigated the police investigation. But they couldn't stop me. Karl even refused to shake hands with me when he left, and the disgust of the rest of the family amounted to more attention than they had ever shown before.

I shall never forget the last Sunday School. All the children sang "Farewell." I bore my testimony full of spirit. My eyes had been opened. I knew Christ lived and with the surety of this knowledge I would ever be obedient to his teachings.

I crossed King's Square in Copenhagen that August morning, going toward the harbor where the ship lay on which I would leave in a few moments. Wearing a thin dress and a little black jacket that I had bought with my postal savings, I kissed my mother goodbye at our home while I still had the courage to do so without weeping. I walked down to the harbor alone. I was frightened, but I felt deeply the ultimate triumph of good over evil. I saw clearly now the way had been prepared in the first twelve years of my life for this spiritual adventure. It will always seem miraculous to me how one situation built upon another until that day of departure: the death of my father, the foster homes, hard work, scripture study in the Danish schools until I was twelve, Oscar and Hilda taking me to their Mormon Sunday School, and finally Elder Willard Hansen from Brigham City, Utah picking me out of several hundred children to return with him to Zion—it had all been preparing me for this day.

Now that glorified moment for which I had fought and struggled had arrived. Yet mine was still the power to choose between the flesh and the spirit. I was still with my mother. I still could stay with her. But I would not falter now; only a coward turns back. It was a decision of immense importance.

I swung myself up the gangplank amidst the waving handkerchiefs of my schoolmates who were bidding me goodbye. I remember standing still, holding on to the railing as the boat glided out into the wide, soft darkness. I stood my ground without a tear until I saw a sweet, tear-stained face come into view. It was my mother. As she squeezed through the crowds, the heat and confusion almost overcame me. I remember whispering through the dark and the stillness, "Oh God, be with us that we may meet again in that land out West, as thou hast promised those who are faithful." It was a child's prayer, and through the whispering of the spirit I felt complete consolation. I was assured that I had done God's will.

At last I was on my way to America. I realized that now everything would be changed. Behind me was my mother, and each movement of the ship told me I was floating further and further from her. I felt seasick. I found my way down a steep narrow stairway into the bottom of the boat. There I found rows of bunk beds on either side and a long table down the center where the emigrants were to eat.

The air was stifling, and

Waving good-bye

there were all kinds of confusion and noise. Little children were crying while mothers were preparing scanty meals. The idea of food made me feel worse. I made my way to one of the bunks, took off my little black jacket, and crawled in. There was little light. At the small windows all I could see was water. I looked around at the darkness and felt the return of bitter reality. But much of the best in life blooms out of its necessities.

I spent every minute of that two-week voyage on my back. I ate nothing because I was so seasick. I saw Elder Hansen only once during the crossing. He

Unloading cargo at Castle Garden, New York

brought me a fresh orange, but I couldn't stand the smell of it. I lay among saints from Sweden, Norway, and several other countries—all heading for Zion. I told myself that, uncomfortable as the situation was, it was only a stepping stone to bigger and better things. I tried to remind myself that it was a return, a spiritual reevaluation, a contrast of temporal things in the light of things eternal. I resolved not to regret my decision to leave my mother and my country. But at the time, none of these thoughts made me feel less homesick or less seasick. . . .

One night my little black jacket was stolen. It was the only covering I had for my body. I had saved so long to buy it that I was heartbroken.

What little fat clung to my bones was gone before we reached New York. Two weeks of seasickness, coupled with an intense longing for my mother, had reduced me to a living skeleton. On the last day of the voyage I finally climbed out of bed for the first time and pulled myself up the narrow stairway. I found myself clinging to the same railing I had clung to on the day of departure.

When the ship glided into New York harbor, a gentle breeze was blowing. Looking up, I saw the morning sun gleaming on the outstretched hand of the Goddess [Statue] of Liberty. She was wonderful to behold—so big, so glorious. I saw her as my new mother welcoming me to America, the land of my new birth. It was a sight I shall never forget. Suddenly, I felt less homesick, and tears of gratitude to God and my church dimmed my eyes.

Members of the Rasmussen family in Denmark before emigrating to America

I saw my first glimpse of America when we landed at Ellis Island [Castle Garden]. Believe me, I couldn't see much except the hundreds of immigrants who were all bigger than I. Jostled by the crowds of people shoving past me, my only thought was to hang on to my belongings. Elder Hansen, who did not have to go through the immigration procedures, had made me responsible for a purebred canary in a bird cage. It had been a gift from the saints in Denmark, and I had promised to carry it safely to Utah. I held the cage in one hand and a two-handled wicker basket containing everything I owned in the other. I must have made a pitiful picture standing alone with my braids hanging down my back. I waited in the din and confusion of the immigrants until my turn finally arrived to be processed.

After a six-day train ride, Valborg arrived in Brigham City, Utah, where she stayed with the Willard Hansen family and worked for them to pay for her immigration.

When that train finally reached its destination and I stepped on to the station platform, there was no one to meet me. I had no idea where to go, so I walked to the nearest house and asked a man, "Where does Willard Hansen live?" I spoke in Danish, but, at that time, Brigham City was full of immigrants. Luckily, he understood me. In no time I had climbed on the man's buckboard and was on my way to the Hansen home.

Elder Hansen's wife, Maria, was holding a quilting bee that day; and when I arrived, still carrying my wicker basket and the canary, she was preparing to serve dinner to the ladies. By that time I was so starved I hurt clear through to my back. I asked Maria if I could have just a crust of bread. She could see how hungry I was, and she fed me. All I ate was a piece of bread and some milk. She would have given me more, but that's all I wanted. It was enough to stop the hunger. I have never been as hungry, before or since, as I was that day.

My first impression of Brigham City was wonderful. It was beautiful. Every home had a little reed organ. To me that was grand. No matter how poor the family, or how bad the adobes looked, the songs of Zion could be heard drifting out of the little houses.

That winter the canary died. Its death was my first real sadness since I had come to America. The cat had eaten it. No one else seemed upset. To them it was just another bird. To me this little companion, whom I had guarded dearly on our long and difficult journey, was the last token of my homeland.

Now its song was ended. Never again would I hear its sweet Danish melody. Enduring the discomforts of my immigration to Zion had not been easy, but this loss was most difficult. With the departure of my tiny yellow friend, I knew I had completed my journey of the heart. But had I? A new song in a new land was all around me, but the echo of the old lingered on and on in my memory.

Valborg lived with the Willard Hansen family, who later moved to Collinston, Utah, where they ran a dairy farm. Her mother and sister later immigrated to Utah with Valborg's hard-earned financial help. They both joined the Church. Valborg married David R. Wheelwright in the Salt Lake Temple, November 28, 1900. They became the parents of four sons, the first of whom died in infancy.

Valborg graduated from Dr. Ellis R. Shipp's School of Obstetrics in 1904 and briefly joined her husband on his mission to Denmark in 1904–1905. She graduated from Weber College, the University of Utah, and was a student at Northwestern University. She was very active in civic musical organizations. She was a member of the Board of Trustees for the School for the Blind and was also a delegate to local and state Republican conventions. She was a candidate for the state legislature and director of employment for women during the Great Depression. She dearly loved music, literature, and painting. She died May 2, 1957, and is buried in the Brigham City Cemetery.

SOURCE: Valborg—An autobiography of Valborg Rasmussen Wheelwright, as told to her son Lorin F. Wheelwright, *20–33. Salt Lake City: Pioneer Music Press, 1978.*

The ship Camoens *carried many Icelandic Latter-day Saints to Liverpool, where they boarded another vessel to cross the Atlantic.*

PART TWO

A Small Village at Sea

"It was a long tedious journey for the old folk, but the youngest did not care so much, for there was something new to be seen all the time."
—Robert Bodily Jr.

Latter-day Saint immigrants who came to America in the nineteenth century spent a long time on the ocean. From 1840 to 1867, the Saints crossed the Atlantic and Pacific Oceans on sailing ships. Relying on the wind to push them to the New World, these ships took about five weeks to travel from Liverpool to New York. It usually took seven to eight weeks to sail from Liverpool to New Orleans. The two longest Latter-day Saint voyages were made by the ship *Frank Johnson,* which brought immigrants from Calcutta, India, to San Francisco in 112 days, and the *Brooklyn,* which took 177 days—nearly six months—to bring a group of over 200 American Saints from New York, around South America, to California.

In 1867, Mormon converts began crossing the ocean in ships powered by steam engines and crossing time was reduced considerably—to an average of ten to twelve days to travel from Liverpool to New York. Still, it took great courage for these young Saints to board a seagoing vessel, knowing something of the dangers that might lie ahead.

Living conditions aboard the ships varied greatly. For some passengers the experience was almost a pleasure cruise. For others it was a terrifying chapter in their lives that they would have liked to forget, but could not. Many factors influenced their enjoyment of the ocean voyage: how many storms they endured, how friendly or gruff the captain and sailors were, what kind of food they had to eat, and whether they were exposed to serious diseases and death aboard the ship.

The histories in this section present experiences young people encountered on emigrant ships in the mid- to late-1800s. The daily events resemble those of a small village of two hundred to nine hundred inhabitants: babies were born, marriages were performed, and funerals were held. There was dancing, singing, and jumping rope; food was prepared and consumed; and the voyagers dealt with illnesses, accidents, and mischief. Amidst it all, they dreamed of the future.

Ann Lydia West and Caroline Eliza West

The Story of Two Sisters

PARENTS: Charles Henry John and Eliza Dangerfield West

SAILING DATE: May 14, 1862[*]

SHIP: *William Tapscott*

Caroline Eliza West (Wright Larrabee)

BORN: December 5, 1851, London, Middlesex, England

AGE: 10

Ann Lydia West (Neville)

BORN: May 1, 1856, London, Middlesex, England

AGE: 6

Later in life, Caroline and Ann wrote separate accounts of their experience of leaving their parents, siblings, and homeland, and crossing the ocean to America. They traveled with the James King family. Here are combined excerpts from their personal histories:

[*] Caroline and Ann sailed on the same voyage as Isabelle Lawrence Price and Ebenezer Farnes. See pages 70 and 75.

nn: My parents joined The Church of Jesus Christ of Latter-day Saints and as the spirit of gathering was so great to get to [America], my parents were anxious to emigrate there. But it was very hard to make a living and save enough to cross the sea and provide for the same. My parents kept an open house for the [Mormon] Elders. A great many stayed with them.

My father was a vellum binder of books. He made a very good living. We all had the comforts of life but no luxuries of life, so that they could not save much.

An Elder was staying with them named John Brown. Elder Brown was full of faith and advised my parents to send some of us children ahead of the family, but they thought they could not do that. A friend of the family by the name of James King and wife came to visit my parents and mother told them of what Elder Brown said. Then, they said "let us take Anna with us as [we are] going [this] year. We love her and will take good care of her." They did not have any children of their own.

I was nearly six then; my older sister about ten years. My parents did not give them an answer at that time, but talked it over with Elder Brown and he said, "send [her] by all means and I will promise you if you keep faithful you will follow the next year."

Anna Andersen, of Odensa, Denmark, dressed up in her finest for a studio picture before sailing to America.

[My parents] thought it over and decided to let me go if they would [also] take my older sister, Caroline. When the Kings came to get their answer [my parents] told them they would let me go if Caroline could go too. They said they would take us both. I remember it quite well, but I wanted my family to go too. The family told us we were going to Zion and the Lord would bless us and they would soon come. We were contented to go.

I remember father taking us on the River Thames and through the tunnel in a large boat. [He took] us to have our pictures taken, one on each side of Father. He also took us to the Castle Garden. I had never before seen green grass grow or living flowers. As soon as I got inside of the gate I looked about me a few minutes and threw myself flat on the grass and spread out my arms. I wanted to hug it and drink it all in my body, it was so grand. I shall never forget it while memory lasts! You see, in London there is no grass or flowers unless it [is] where the wealthy live.

Caroline: Sometime in the month of May 1862, when the emigrants started on their journey, we left London in the morning. I remember leaving father, mother, brothers and sister. Did I cry? No. I was going to Zion. Did my sister cry? I don't remember that she did. We got to Liverpool in good time, and got on the ship.

Ann: Mother said that if she could of called the ship back, she surely would have done it. She had not realized what it meant until that big ship sailed way out of sight and maybe [she would] never see us again. But she remembered the promise made [to] them, so [she] went home and worked harder than ever making shirts and fancy boxes, which was her trade, to help get money to pay their passage to America.

Caroline: It was a three-masted sailing ship. It had three decks, the top deck where you could look over the side and see the ocean, then you went down a trapdoor to the second deck. This was like a large room with berths built all around the walls of the ship. They were the places you slept in. There were three tiers, one of them above the other. Then there was another trapdoor that let you down into another deck. When you got on the floor of the third deck, it was so dark that you could not see for awhile till your eyes got accustomed to the gloom. On the third floor were more berths all around, and some lanterns lit so you could manage to see around. The berths that Brother King and family and we two children had were down in this lowest deck.

Gerda Caroline Johansen, of Denmark, before her voyage to America

The rations consisted of sea biscuits that were as large as a modern-sized plate and were hollow. There was salt beef, pork, rice, split peas, oatmeal, vinegar, mustard, black tea, brown sugar, fresh water and a very little flour, for there was no way of baking bread. The flour was to make a pie or pudding if you wanted to. Brother King used to take the meat and the food to the cooking galley and get it cooked. Lots of the people had some extra food stuffs with them

Passengers eating in the galley of a vessel

The children make themselves happy, both above and below deck. Marbles, skipping ropes, and all the available paraphernalia of childhood's games are called into request. The older boys amuse themselves by tugging at the ropes with the sailors. So merrily we live together.

—*John Jaques emigrated at age 29, in 1856, aboard the Horizon.*

such as raisins, currants, and other fancy stuff. Brother King used to make gruel of the oatmeal and cook other things. The reason he had to do this was because his wife and his sisters were sick and his mother was old.

Ann: It was so strange to see the water all around us. When the sun went down—I was wild. I said, "the sun will be drowned and will never come up again." I jumped up and down and wrung my hands in despair. A man standing near me said, "don't worry, it will come up again." Then we were ordered down in the hold of the ship. It was terrible down there. It smelled bad and was dark. We had eight weeks of that horrible bad food. It consisted of hard tack, oatmeal hulls and all. No milk, no sugar—very [little] salt beef.

Caroline: My sister and I were not sick. We would get two of those big sea biscuits each with a piece of boiled beef and pork with some mustard and vinegar on it, and go up on the upper deck and sit on the coils of rope enjoying ourselves. Then we would prowl around poking our noses into every place we got a chance. We managed to find out where the captain's cook was cooking and he wanted to know if we could sing. We said yes, so he asked us to sing for him, which we did. He gave us some nice fresh meat, broth, bread, cake and many other good things. We took some of it to Sister King for she was so sick.

The only place I was frightened was when we had to go to the closet [bathroom], there was just a straight stick across and of course you could see the ocean [below]. How I did cling to my little sister when she was on that bar, for it was a large enough place to let a grown person down, let alone children.

Ann: The only pleasure we had was when they would let us go on deck and we would look out at the sea and we would see large fishes, porpoises and others. We liked to see the animals and chickens they had in coops around the deck.

Caroline: We had an awful storm. How the ship did rock! It seemed like it would tip over, and how the cans and things did tumble around; but we got to New York all right. We stopped in a place called Castle Garden, it was a large building. I have read since that it had been built for an Opera House and used for that, and the great singer Jenny Lind sang there. We stayed a few days at Castle Garden then we got on the [railroad] cars, and how hungry we were. We bought bread from men who came on the cars with bread to sell and it was like eating wind, there was nothing to it or substantial about it. How we

As soon as we got on board the steamer, I noticed an officer motioning to me, I thought. Father stood by me; he told me to go over to the officer and see what he wanted. I did, and he asked, "Is your father here?" "Yes, Sir," I replied. He asked Father if he had a ticket for me. Father said "yes, his is a steerage passage, the same as ours." The officer said, "If you will let this boy work across, we will give the whole family first cabin food for his pay." I was surely a tickled boy. I was dressed in a big white apron. We were nine days from Liverpool to New York. The hand of providence was surely with us for our dear mother's sake, having the very best of food to eat, for she wasn't very well, the trip being quite tiresome.

—*Thomas William Frederick Allen emigrated at age 12, in 1871, aboard the* Minnesota.

From 1853 to 1854, the Golconda *carried 785 Latter-day Saints across the Atlantic on two different voyages.*

We had the pleasure to see a wedding [at] sea. The bride was tied to a chair. She was hoisted up the mast quite a ways. The captain said what a brave woman. Then she took her handkerchief and waved it in the breeze. The brides-man was carried around the ship in a chair by four bachelors. They made it for that purpose. This took place about the first of March, 1854.

—John Johnson Davies emigrated at age 22, in 1854, aboard the Golconda.

did wish for some of the sea biscuits to fill up on. We rode on the cars a while then we got on steamboats and were packed in them like sardines in a can. Thirsty, oh how thirsty, we were on the Missouri River. When they would dip up a bucketful of water and let it settle, it was half sand, and how warm it was. Finally we got to Florence where we stayed two weeks while they were getting the oxen and wagons ready.

Ann: We started on our long journey across the Plains. Brother King started [the trip] with his mother, wife and sister. Sister King gave birth to a baby boy. It was premature. It died, and the next day Sister King passed away, and in a short time Brother King's mother died. They buried them by the road.

We had to walk a great deal of the way. The only time we rode was when [the drivers of] a freight wagon, which was the one ahead of us, would tell us we could ride with them if we would sing for them. How we would sing all the songs we knew. I thought I had to earn my ride. I was very glad that our father had taught us to sing. We, my sister and myself, sang in a concert before we left England and were applauded.

We arrived in Salt Lake City on the first of October, [1862]. [Our parents] heard we arrived in America all right. [They] worried very much and worked hard so they could emigrate the year after we left. One night nearly a year after we left my mother dreamed she saw us and we looked so thin and ragged and dirty she woke up crying and told father her dream. He consoled her the best he could and told her the promises made by the elders, so she went to sleep again and dreamed that she saw us fat and well, our long hair cut short and dressed in grey home spun dresses and looked so happy that she said she never worried again for us.

One day I was playing with playmates in an unfinished room in the Bishop's house [in Provo] and I remembered I was dressed in Aunt Sarah's* clothes. She came to me and said, "Would you like to see your mother?" and I said "Yes, where is she?" I looked out of the window and I saw a covered wagon out there. I knew my parents had come. I pulled off my dress of Aunty's and ran out and there sure enough was my father and mother, but I hardly knew them. They were so travel-stained. I [had] always [seen] them dressed so nice.

When the sea was calm we could occupy our time in reading, sewing, and taking our walk on deck. Also listening to the sailors singing while they were pumping the water out from the bottom of the ship. They never worked without singing, so they could all pull together. Then it was a grand sight to see the sun go down.

—*Elizabeth White Stewart emigrated at age 18, in 1856, aboard the* Horizon.

---

* Aunt Sarah was the bishop's wife. She was no relation to Ann or Caroline.

Caroline married Thomas Henry Wright on February 8, 1869, and they became the parents of five children. They lived in Summit County, Utah. After Thomas died in 1881, she married Thomas Jefferson Larrabee. Caroline received a blessing from a Mormon missionary in England when she was just two weeks old. She was promised that in her young days she would be "gathered to Zion and be a mother in Israel." That promise was fulfilled in every way.

Ann married Joseph Hyrum Neville in 1873. He was a blacksmith, bricklayer, and plasterer, and did brick and plaster work for the Salt Lake Theater, schools, courthouses, and churches. Ann frequently cooked for the men her husband worked with. Ann and Joseph became the parents of ten children. They lived in Woodruff, Bountiful, and Ogden, Utah. Ann enjoyed participating in community plays and musical productions and faithfully served the Church in nearly every auxiliary. She and her husband were later called to settle in Big Horn County, Wyoming. There the Neville family helped dig canals, installed telegraph and telephone lines, and ran a store. Ann died true to the faith on July 14, 1930, in Byron, Wyoming.

SOURCES: Larrabee, Caroline E. W. W. Autobiography. In Our Pioneer Heritage, compiled by Kate B. Carter. 17:290–92. Salt Lake City: Daughters of Utah Pioneers, 1974. Also "Biography of Ann L. West Neville," written January 1929. In private possession of Marilyn H. Mecham, Salt Lake City, Utah.

Percy Groom

"Our meager rations dwindled to none."

BORN: January 29, 1874, Greengate, Salford, Lancaster, England
PARENTS: Nathan and Emma Elizabeth Hill Groom
SAILING DATE: May 16, 1885
SHIP: *Wisconsin*
AGE: 11

Like many other newly converted Latter-day Saint families, the Grooms were unable to afford to come to Zion all in the same year. Percy's brother emigrated to Utah in 1883; his father emigrated in 1884; and, in 1885, Percy, his mother, and his brother made the long journey.

ne bright May morning in the early eighties, mother, my brother Nathan Jr., and myself left so-called merry England for Utah. Mother had sold all the goods and chattels she wanted to sell, and some not being [sellable], she gave them away or left them in the house for

Between 1872–1890, the Wisconsin *carried nearly 9,000 emigrating Saints from Liverpool to America.*

We danced on the deck. The captain would often amuse himself by throwing nice small cakes and see us scramble to see who would get them. We were divided into four wards on the ship and a president for each. Our worst trouble was [our lack of] appetite. Father was the only one that could eat the sea biscuits so when we reached America we had lots of them. I think we sold them when we got ashore.

—*Isaac Sorensen emigrated at age 16, in 1857, aboard the Westmoreland.*

others to use. However, mother had some nice china tea sets and some Dresden ware and other bric-a-brac that she neither would sell or give away, and other heirlooms that were dear to the heart of English women.

Things went well at the start. We boarded the good ship *Wisconsin* at Liverpool [along] with about 300 other emigrating Saints from Denmark, Sweden, Norway, Germany, Holland and other parts of the British Isles. We started across the mighty deep. The old ship was a rather rickety tub and it was in the habit of twisting, yawning, squeaking and groaning as it made its way against the buffeting of the waves, but the Saints were going to Zion, and they made the welkin [heavens] ring with their Mormon songs. Strange, but all these nationalities could sing the piece; that is, the tune was the same, but the words were expressed differently. But what [they] lacked in unison of words, they made up in the rendition of such songs as: "Come, Come, Ye Saints," "We Thank Thee, Oh God, for a Prophet," and "Israel, Israel, God is Calling," etc.

The trip was quite exciting seeing whales, porpoises and other marine animals and birds. It is strange how long a flock of seagulls will follow a ship and keep up with it without resting a spell. Some thirty large icebergs were seen on the way. May is a good time to cross if one wants to see these dull, silent, gray piles of arctic glaciers as they majestically float down from Greenland and eventually melt in the Gulf Stream. One large pile of ice had as a passenger a polar bear. This [cub] was no doubt beyond his depths, [and] when the iceberg melted, which it surely would do, then the bear would be without a footing. And while very clever in water, [he would] have to come up for breathing, and eventually the poor bear would become a victim of its own thoughtlessness. It took a total of thirty days to cross the Atlantic.

The immigrant passengers on the ship *Wisconsin* crowded the deck, everyone pushing to the rail, jostling one another to get their first glimpse of America. Mothers lifted their small children to a better vantage point. The Statue of Liberty lifted her torch to the new residents entering New York Harbor. Each member of the family read the inscription on the base of the giant lady which reads, in part: "Give me your tired, your poor, your huddled masses yearning to breathe free, the wretched refuse of your teaming shore, send these the homeless, tempest tossed, to me: I lift my lamp beside the golden door." . . .

My mother never thought that [the American customs agents would be] so keen-nosed to search through her baggage. They spied the sets of china, the Dresden plate and other bric-a-brac

We were on the Atlantic eleven weeks and three days, and had very little to eat. They gave each of us a tin plate, tin cup, and a spoon when we started and we kept them as our own. Then a man came around with two large pails, one in each hand, and gave us our rations. Every other day we had split peas boiled without seasoning, and often burnt at that. The next day we had barley prepared for food, and boiled the same way. The grown people had one cup each day, us children half a cup. Then we had what they called sea-biscuits. They were as large as a small saucer and were made of shorts or some course meal of some kind, and so hard we could only gnaw them, but we were glad to get the one each for the grown-ups and the one-half for children.

—*Maren Jensen Cutler Norton emigrated at age 7, in 1853, aboard the* Forest Monarch.

and immediately put the usual tariff charges against it. This placed her in a position to either leave her precious goods in the hands of the government or pay the charges; she chose the latter. However, this almost cleaned her out of our passage money to buy food from New York to Salt Lake City. After shelling out to "Uncle Sam," she had in American money the sum of $1.96 to keep herself and two boys in food from [New York] to Zion.

Customs completed, we made our way to Grand Central Station in New York to board the train for the four day trip to Utah. With good [Scottish] thrift, mother made the $1.96 go as far as it could, but even then our food consisted of water from the tap, bread, and canned meat. The train journey seemed long and our meager rations dwindled to none. No more food became available until the morning after our arrival in Buttlerville Bench, east of Murray, Utah. I was so hungry and my stomach hurt so badly I was unable to sleep my first night in Zion.

The Groom family settled in the Holliday area of the Salt Lake Valley and farmed. They moved to the Snake River Valley in eastern Idaho in 1887. There they homesteaded a piece of land that had sagebrush six feet tall. Percy married Adella Short in 1898, and they became the parents of five children. Percy studied law and became a successful self-taught attorney. He was admitted to the Idaho State Bar Association in 1914. He later moved his family to Rigby, Idaho, where he was elected probate judge of Jefferson County. In 1927 he established a private law practice, retiring in 1954. Percy lived a short distance from his law office, and every day he would walk back and forth to work, whistling all the way. His whistle could be heard for some distance and many knew him as "The Whistling Judge." He died July 27, 1958, in Idaho Falls, Idaho.

SOURCE: *Groom, Percy. Biographical Sketch, 3–5. LDS Church Archives.*

The 1853 voyage of the International *recorded seven deaths, seven births, five marriages, and forty-eight baptisms, which included the captain, first and second mates, and eighteen of the crew.*

Stephen Forsdick *

"I was dead broke and had holes in the toes of my shoes."

BORN: October 8, 1835, Watford, Hertfordshire, England
PARENTS: Unknown
SAILING DATE: February 28, 1853
SHIP: *International*
AGE: 17

In February 1853, I received word that the ship *International* would sail on the twenty-third and for me to be in Liverpool on the eighteenth. The winter had been very mild and I had enjoyed myself in hunting and visiting around with my friends and relatives. Snow fell about the middle of the month and was on the ground when I received notice to go.

I made my farewell visits and spent the evening of the seventeenth at home with my father and mother. The next morning before they were up, I kissed them all goodbye and that same evening arrived in Liverpool.

The next few days were spent in getting our berths on board the ship, getting

* No picture of Stephen Forsdick is currently known to be available.

After we got out in the sea, the people began to be seasick. I do not think . . . ten escaped and I was one of the favored ones. I was not sick a half hour all the voyage through. We had a very pleasant trip. We had dancing and music every evening, with a very few exceptions. Our regular meetings were held, and we had a splendid party on the captain's birthday. The young people got up a nice program for the day.

—*Fanny Fry Simons emigrated at age 16, in 1859, aboard the* William Tapscott.

our luggage on board, paying our fare and getting all necessary tinware, mattresses, etc. to use on shipboard.

My mother had given me a pail for water, a pair of blankets and some other things, so that I had only to get a mattress—and a very poor one it proved to be. The tinware which was bought was of the cheapest sort and was worn out long before we reached our destination.

Our party was composed of an old man named John Doggett, three young ladies, Misses Rosa [A.] and Nancy [M.] Orrell, Eliza Hester [Esther] and myself. When it came time to pay for the passage, none of them seemed to have enough money and all borrowed from me. I loaned them altogether about thirty dollars and I think that five dollars was all of it that I ever saw again. As a consequence, when I arrived at my journey's end, I was dead broke and had holes in the toes of my shoes.

Lise Rasmussen and her brother Sorn of Denmark before emigrating

On the twenty-fifth day of February, the ship was towed out of the dock into the River Mersey and dropped anchor. We remained here two days, while all were ordered on deck, answered to our names and were examined by a doctor before the ship could get her clearance papers.

While we were anchored an old gentleman from Wales died and was taken ashore for burial.

Our organization was then accomplished. Christopher Arthur from Newport was appointed president and John Lyons [Lyon] and Richard Waddington counselors and Elder [George] Sims as clerk. The bunks were divided into wards, with a president over each and others were appointed to see that the beds were made and everything kept clean and neat during the voyage.

A watch was appointed to see that all hands were in their bunks by ten o'clock at night. We had three London policemen on board and they were assigned to police duty. . . .

Most of us were in the steerage. A few were in what was called the second cabin, for which something more was paid, but after we were out to sea, the steerage proved to be the better ventilated and the more comfortable of the two.

While on shipboard, we children were bathed in big tubs and barrels of sea water, which we did not fancy. Many people were on board, and the weather was very cold. One day I was sitting on a little stool near a stove. A woman with a baby wanted the stool, so she pulled it from under me, causing me to fall against the stove and my hand was so badly burned that the scar remains to this day.

—*Ann Jane Willden Johnson emigrated at age 4, in January 1849, aboard the* Zetland.

Thorvald C. C. Larsen of Denmark

I think that we drew our rations, consisting of hardtack, rice, tea, sugar, salt, beef or pork once a week. We [were] given four quarts of water each day and had to get it early in the morning.

As soon as we were organized we commenced a routine which was about as follows: up at daylight and get breakfast. Then came morning prayers in all the wards, then it was sweep and clean up. After that we could promenade on deck, sing or do whatever we chose until time to get dinner.

The cooking was done by two young men in a little house on deck called the galley. . . . The meat was all boiled together, each person tying a wooden or tin tag with his name or the number of this berth on it to his piece. Rice was tied in a bag and cooked the same way.

If a person wanted anything fried or cooked in any other way, they would have to wait their turn. Most of the passengers took fresh meat, fresh bread, butter and many other things with them, so that we didn't suffer for anything to eat.

On the twenty-seventh day of February after breakfast, the ship weighed anchor and a tug took her in tow, down the river several miles.

I was below sweeping at the time, but soon went on deck. While the tug had hold of us, the ship settled down to business and so did most of the passengers.

At first we were a little dizzy, then sick at the stomach. The crowd on deck soon thinned out and by night a large part of the human cargo was learning what it was to be seasick and the next ten days were lost time to me.

The first morning at sea was a little rough and some of the timid ones thought the ship would sink. I remember some of the sailors came downstairs to stow away the anchor chains, and someone asked them if it was not dangerous that way the ship was rolling. One of the sailors made reply, "If it keeps this up for twenty-four hours the catfish will be eating you," while in fact, there was no danger at all, but a sailor, like a cowboy, likes to play it off on a tenderfoot.

Crowded conditions below deck

During the first week or so, the cooks had an easy time of it, very few having much appetite and the deck was not crowded. I used to crawl up on deck and get my arms through the ratline and try to throw up my boots. My best description of seasickness is that, the first day or two you are afraid you are going to die; the rest of the time, you don't care how soon you do. All things come to an end, however, and so did seasickness to most of us and then we fell into our regular routine again.

We had contrary winds nearly all the way. After we had been out of port six weeks, the captain said that he could sail back to Liverpool in six days and said that if the wind did not change within a week, we would have to go on short rations until we did. Maybe you don't think there was some earnest praying done for the wind to change, as it was a characteristic of the Mormon religion to pray for the thing needed at the time, so that all our prayers now were that God would change the wind and bring us all safe home to Zion.

Well, whether the Lord changed the wind or not, I do not know, but the day before our rations were to be served out, we found in the morning when we awoke that we had fair winds and plenty of it, the ship was going through the water like a race horse.

On the sixth day of April, that being the anniversary of the organization of the Mormon Church, it was decided to celebrate the day in grand style on shipboard. Committees were appointed and a big program arranged. After marching and counter-marching across the deck, the assembly was called to order by the president, and singing, recitations and speeches were the order of the day.

We had some splendid singers on board and some pretty fair poets, and with original and selected songs and recitations, the day passed

There were no bathrooms or toilets. Each family was given a slop pail shaped like a stove pipe hat. They were called "Tin Hats." When not in use they were hung from nails from the ceiling. When it was calm it was fine. But when a storm came up they said the banging and clatter from the "Tin Hats" was terrible.

—*Henry Bolton emigrated at age 20, in 1866, aboard the American Congress.*

Andrew Martin Israelsen

Andrew Martin Israelsen left his homeland of Norway at the age of 7 and crossed the Atlantic Ocean with his family in 1864. During the voyage, he became very ill and was declared dead by a doctor aboard the ship. The doctor ordered the boy's body thrown overboard. However, Andrew's father pleaded with the ship crew to wait, and within a short time Andrew showed signs of life and soon fully recovered. Andrew made it safely to Utah and settled in Cache Valley. He became the father of ten children and lived to the age of 82.

very pleasantly. While we were in the midst of our celebration, we passed close to another large ship homeward bound. After the wind changed we made our way rapidly to the south and west, the weather getting much warmer.

The women folk went to work making tents and wagon covers. The ducking [a heavy cotton fabric] from which they were made having been brought from England. One or two men did the cutting and the rest did the sewing. I think about twenty-five tents and wagon covers were made.

About this time some of the sailors wanted to be baptized and the captain had a large tank brought on deck for the purpose. It was later used for a bathtub, so that anyone wishing to take a bath in sea water could do so. The captain was the first to be baptized. He was followed by the second mate, then the sailors and the rest of the officers, until by the time we reached New Orleans the captain, the second mate and the entire crew, with one exception, belonged to the Mormon Church. The carpenter, second mate, and several of the sailors went through to Salt Lake with us. . . .

Ours had been a remarkable voyage. Other ships had baptized a few sailors, but to convert the entire crew, with just one exception, was something that had never happened before.

About the seventeenth of April we sighted land. It was the Great Abasko, one of the West India Islands, at what was called "The Hole in the Wall." The channel is quite narrow at that place and I remember soon after that we passed two coral reefs, called the "Big and the Little Isaac's." . . .

Without any accident, about the twenty-fourth of April, we arrived at the mouth of the Mississippi River. . . .

When we arrived at the mouth of the river, the water instead of being nearly green became yellow. The sailor told us it was the Mississippi River and was fresh and fit to drink which we found to be true.

Here a tug took hold of us and towed us over the bar, then took another vessel on the other side of her and we proceeded up the river without dropping anchor.

The land on either side of the river for some distance was low and swampy, but as we neared New Orleans orange groves began to appear and it was quite a sight to us to see ripe and green fruit and blossoms on the trees at the same time. I think it was on the evening of the twenty-fourth of April, that we tied up at the levee in New Orleans, having made the trip in about nine weeks.

We had no sickness except seasickness, had one marriage [and] two or three births, so that we arrived with more on board than we had when we started.

After traveling to Utah with the Latter-day Saints, Stephen apparently returned to live in the Midwest. Stephen married Lucinda Melissa Davenport, who was born in Farmington, Michigan, on July 1, 1838. Stephen died January 29, 1927, at the age of ninety-one. He is buried in Chester, Nebraska.

SOURCE: Forsdick, Stephen. Autobiography, 10–14: Duplication of typescript. LDS Church Archives. Note: Some paragraphs have been rearranged for clarity.

George Isom

"I could not recollect having ever previously been more than eight or ten miles from home."

BORN: August 17, 1846, England
PARENTS: Owen and Elizabeth Howard Isom
SAILING DATE: May 11, 1860
SHIP: *William Tapscott*
AGE: 13

I shall not forget my feelings when standing upon the docks at Liverpool and looking forth upon the mighty waters. The chilly sea breeze seemed to penetrate my very bones and cause a shrinking feeling of fear to come over me, but this was soon dispelled by the novelty of the scene, as I could not recollect having ever previously been more than eight or ten miles from home and had never seen a ship or stream or body of water larger than a brook before.

Here I was in sight of hundreds of vessels, both sail and steam, with tow and other smaller craft in great numbers, while at the docks and through the town the bustle and thrift caused by the commerce of the sea was everywhere visible.

After looking around awhile, a towboat drew up alongside the wharf upon which we thronged with our luggage to be conveyed to the vessel, which stood out from the shore some distance at anchor. We soon reached the side of the ship, a most noble looking vessel. Previous to embarking, while yet upon the towboat, [the ship] appeared to be as high as a three-story house, but when the passengers, one thousand in number, were all aboard, it settled down in the water considerably.

Captain [James B.] Bell proved very kind and gentlemanly in bearing toward our people. As soon as we were all aboard, the sailors weighed anchor and the

Leaving Liverpool

[tow]boat, though considerably smaller . . . caused us to glide easily and rapidly through the water.

Toward morning, upon awakening, we found that our vessel had ceased to glide smoothly. Our little champion, the towboat, had left us to fate, and we

I forgot to say anything about trying to wash my shirt. I had seen mother washing and I commenced and thought I could do the same. I rubbed until I rubbed the skin off my knuckles and then I tied my shirt with a rope and threw it overboard and that was all the washing that I done. We also seen the little flying fish and some of them fell on our deck, they were about five inches long and cannot fly far.

—*James Moyle emigrated at age 18, in 1854, aboard the* John Wood.

rolled and pitched considerably, disturbing the equilibrium of a great number of the passengers' stomachs. What a deplorable set of beings. We appeared to be nearly all sick and, of course, few to give sympathy.

My father, fortunately, was not troubled by the rolling of the vessel, so he had to practice the art of cookery for himself and the rest of us when we could eat, although we all soon recovered with the exception of Samuel. He did not fully recover for two or three weeks.

We were five weeks upon the sea. This was a long time to be confined with[in] the narrow limits of a sailing vessel, although the life on the ocean wave was new and novel to us and we were diverted by watching the sailors and hearing them sing, "Haul, haul away, haul away Jo." And then upon reaching the word "Jo" all pulling together. [It was the same] with many other sailor rhymes. . . .

We occasionally saw shoals of porpoises which came gambolling upon the surface of the deep and when on account of unfavorable winds we were compelled to take to the north to make headway, we saw jets of water, occasionally rising several feet above the otherwise smooth surface of the ocean. We watched anxiously for a glimpse of the whale, but Mr. Whale failed to show anything but his locality at breathing time.

We Latter-day Saints did not forget our God amidst the excitement and curiosities of an ocean voyage, but our hearts and voices were ever turned to him in prayer and praise, and we were blessed and prospered upon the seas.

We escaped all dangers, and although [we were] many in number I do not remember more than two or three being rolled up in canvas and slid off a plank into the watery grave.

Notwithstanding the novelty of a sea voyage to one traveling over its bosom for the first time, we were very joyful when we beheld the low, misty outlines of Long Island. But upon reaching the quarantine grounds we were not permitted to go ashore on account of two or three Danish persons being sick with small-pox. We were much chagrined, although we did not tire of looking upon the scenery upon either side of the river—the beautiful green sloping shore studded with suburban residences making a most enchanting scene to us voyagers. The sick were removed to Blackwell, or Mare Island, situated between New York and Brooklyn on the East River, and [we] were permitted to go ashore. As we embarked so we disembarked, by means of a towboat.

We landed at Castle Garden, a place prepared for the reception of emigrants where they can remain a day or two until they find more suitable quarters. The most of our brethren being bound for Salt Lake City, continued their journey by rail.

George married Alice Parker in 1869 in the Salt Lake Endowment House, and they became the parents of nine children. They settled in Southern Utah in Washington County. George worked hard and supported his family in a variety of ways. He farmed, made shoes, sold grapes, did freighting, built houses and cellars, and ran a cane mill from which he made thousands of gallons of molasses. His family lived the United Order from 1875 to 1877.

At the age of thirty-nine, George became ill while traveling in cold weather to and from St. George and died on December 6, 1885, at Virgin, Utah. His ninth child was born two weeks after his death. The two-story rock home George built for his family in Virgin was still standing at the arrival of the new millennium in the year 2000.

SOURCE: Isom, George. Memories of George Isom, 5–9. Typescript. LDS Church Archives.

Isabelle Kunkel holding her son Mark

Isabelle Lawrence Price (Kunkel)

"How happy everybody was!"

BORN: September 9, 1847, Birmingham, Warwick, England
PARENTS: Edward and Matilda Lawrence Price
SAILING DATE: May 14, 1862
SHIP: *William Tapscott*
AGE: 14

The following is part of a letter Isabelle Price Kunkel wrote in her later years to her daughter Nellie May Price Doran, telling of her voyage to America:

My dear Nellie May,

A few items or incidents that may be interesting to you that happened during our long journey to Utah, our grand old mountain home. I can't remember the time when the place was not talked about in our home, for we always planned to come sometime. At last the time did really come.

70

On Monday, the 14th day of May 1862, we left Birmingham for Liverpool, England, and went directly on board the ship, *William Tapscott,* commanded by Captain Bell (if I remember right, his name was William Bell).* He was a fine man, bluff and ruddy but kindly and every inch a man. It was his third or fourth trip across the ocean with a shipload of Mormons, and he told my father that he never felt so safe or had better voyages than when he was bringing over a ship load of Latter-day Saints.

This time there were eight hundred and fifty souls on board, including the crew. It was a sailing vessel depending entirely on the wind and sails to carry us across that big blue sea. We set sail about eight o'clock that same evening. How happy everyone was! As the ship began to move, hundreds of voices—men, women and children—began to sing: Come, Come Ye Saints; then Cheer Saints, Cheer, We Are Bound for Peaceful Zion, Cheer Saints Cheer for the Free and Happy Land; then Oh Ye Mountains High in the Clear Blue Sky, by Charles W. Penrose. It was one of the nights that I have never forgotten.

We were second-cabin passengers, the only accommodation to be had. Our cabin was a room with four berths in it. The light was from a large porthole covered with very thick blue glass. When the sea was not too rough, we had it open. [My brother] Lorenzo used to always have a heavy fish line hanging out always hoping to land a big fish, but he never did. Our family consisted at that time of Father, Edward Price; Mother, Matilda Lawrence Price; and six children: Lorenzo age 16, Agnes 13, Walter 12, Linda 3, Eli 14 months, and myself, Isabelle, 14 years.

For weeks we were on the Atlantic Ocean. As we children played around, sometimes we stood and watched the cooks kill chickens by wringing their necks. This seemed horrible to me. But afterwards I remember how good the chicken bones tasted that we picked up after the sailors had thrown them away.

—Mary Ann Hafen emigrated at age 6, in 1860, aboard the Underwriter.

* The captain of the voyage was James B. Bell.

We sailed on an old wooden vessel called *Alacrity*. We had not been sailing long before something began to happen. We began to be sick and sick we surely were, but in a few days we began to recover and our appetites could hardly be satisfied. We were hungry all the time.

—*Robert Bodily emigrated at age 15, in 1860, aboard the* Alacrity.

[Our sister] Matilda had come the year before in the care of some friends. She was 18 years.

There was a row of cabins similar to ours on each side of the ship, not all as large. They were numbered—ours was No. 1. In the center of the ship there were two long tables running down as far as the cabins reached. On each side of the table, long benches were secured safely to the floor. We had to do our own cooking. There was what they call a cooking galley. The stove in it was about ten feet square with a space about three feet all around it for the people to stand and hold on to their pans and sauce pans, for they would sometimes slide all over the stove, if the sea was a bit rough. That was my first initiation in cooking. Mother was seasick for two weeks. The night we set sail I don't remember that we had any supper; we had been too busy all day and too excited to think of eating.

It was lots of fun the next day to watch the sailors stow away the baggage for so many people. We youngsters all around the hatchways were watching them lower the trunks from the deck into the hold when all at once a little boy, a Welsh boy, leaned too far over and lost his balance and came tumbling down three stories to the hold. He just missed me. He almost struck me in the face as he passed the place where I was leaning over looking over too, to see all I could. It was a wonder it did not kill the poor child. It broke his leg in two places. They put him in a cabin opposite ours. He was such a patient, jolly little fellow. When his leg did not pain him he used to sing: "Put Your Shoulder to the Wheel is a Motto for Every Man." He would sing at the top of his voice the chorus: "Drive care away, for

The William Tapscott *carried more Mormon immigrants to Zion than any other sailing vessel, totaling 2,262 LDS passengers on three voyages.*

grieving is a folly. Put your shoulder to the wheel is a motto for every man." That was our only accident during our trip on the ocean. Three babies died and were buried in the sea.

In the early part of June, we were in a dead calm for three days. The sailors said we had only traveled about three or four miles a day. It seemed so funny not to be moving after making a good headway. It gave us a queer feeling to be so still. The sea was just as calm as a pan of water, not a ripple to be seen. Our ship had [previously] been traveling from 11 to 14 knots an hour.

Then on the 21st of June we had a terrific storm of wind and rain. The waves were mountain high. As one end of the ship went down, you could not see over the top of the waves, the next minute the other would be down. It was the grandest sight that I ever saw, beautiful but awful in its grandeur. But havoc in the steerage and in our quarters too. The buckets, grips, pans and all kinds of cooking utensils and trunks were skating all over the place. A great many of the women and children were frightened nearly to death. Some felt sure we would be shipwrecked. It was after this awful storm that Captain Bell told my father he always felt perfectly safe when he had our people on board. There was no thought of cooking that day for no one was allowed on deck, but strange to say, we did not think of food or eating; not even the children [did]. About the 24th of June we arrived in New York and bid farewell to kind Captain Bell.

The Price family crossed the Plains with the Horton D. Haight Company, arriving in the Salt Lake Valley on October 19, 1862. Isabelle (known as "Belle") married Francis "Frank" Smith in 1868, who worked for the Woodmansee Brothers Mercantile store in Salt Lake City. They had one child. Frank died in 1869, at the age of twenty-six, from injuries sustained in a fall.

Belle then married Solomon F. Kunkel in 1873. Solomon was a mine owner, and they lived for a short time in Reno, Nevada. They returned to Salt Lake City in 1875, where they raised their family of nine children. Belle was a talented dressmaker, a skill she learned from her mother. She was also an excellent cook. Her children especially enjoyed the special mince pies and flaming plum puddings she served as desserts for Christmas dinner. Belle was a widow for fourteen years before she died September 2, 1930. She was eighty-three years old.

SOURCE: Kunkel, Isabelle Price. "An Historic Letter." In Our Pioneer Heritage, compiled by Kate B. Carter, 7:260–62. Salt Lake City: Daughters of Utah Pioneers, 1964.

Ebenezer Farnes

"An old tub . . . good enough to carry Mormons on."

BORN: February 4, 1843, Dagenham, Essex, England
PARENTS: John Burnside and Ann Isacke Farnes
SAILING DATE: May 14, 1862
SHIP: *William Tapscott*
AGE: 19

When I was] about nineteen years old in 1862, I emigrated for America on the ship *[William] Tapscott* with 852 passengers. This ship was a three-mast sailing vessel, old and worn out; an old tub not fit for merchandise, but good enough to carry the Mormons on. The ship was eight weeks and two days crossing the ocean. Before I left London I had five young girls put in my charge to see that they got through all safe. Their names were Jane Seamon, Eliza Pinnock, Emma Spencer, Fanny Penny, and one more. When on board the ship I had five more put under my charge, Mrs. [Sarah] White and her four children.

The first day out of the harbor all the emigrants were seasick and I was

* Ebenezer sailed on the same voyage as Caroline and Ann West and Isabelle Lawrence Price. See pages 47 and 70.

After we commenced to get over our seasickness, Emily Harris and I used to walk together along the passageway between the ship's cook shops, bakery, where the food was cooked for the captain, first and second class passengers, and where the waiters used to load their trays. . . . One of the waiters used to give us fancy cookies and cakes from his tray in passing us. . . . It was like walking along the main street of a city. . . . I remember the smell of roasting meat and other foods, and one shop where five or six men peeled all the potatoes all day long. But potatoes for the third class steerage people were served with their skins on. Now, in the year 1931, this is thought to be the best way to cook potatoes from a health point of view, but then this was thought to be the way to cook them for fattening hogs.

—*Emma Neat Bennett emigrated at age 10, in June 1879, aboard the* Wyoming.

called on to help give out water and provisions, which I did until we landed in New York. The trip on the ocean was a red letter day in my life. The first day out was rather rough and the second day rougher, and all the people were seasick. After the fourth day out things on board ship went smooth and some of the people came on deck. Others lay in their berths afraid they would die, and others afraid they wouldn't die.

About the third week on the voyage there came a terrible storm which tore everything down that could be broken. So bad was the storm that the people had to stay in their beds for three days, the hatchway being closed most of the time, the water being one foot [deep] on the first and second decks, washing from one end of the ship to the other and side to side, as the ship tossed and rolled. The captain said it was the worst storm he had ever seen and he had been a captain for twenty-five years. The ship sprung a leak and the pumps had to be kept going night and day until we reached New York. When the captain was asked about the storm he said if he had known the condition of the ship he would not have sailed on her, but consoled himself [that] as he had a load of "Mormons" on board he would get through all right, as there had never been a ship lost that was carrying "Mormons." After the ship landed in New York, she was not considered fit to carry anything back but lumber so they loaded her with that and she water-logged and was lost at sea.

Taking the voyage all in all, it was quite an experience for us all. Only two deaths, one child and a man who was sick when he came on board. The burial at sea is a sad thing. The body is sewn in a canvas and a ball of iron placed at their feet so as to make the body sink feet first so the sharks cannot get it. A long plank is placed on the rail of the ship, part on the ship and part over the water, and the body is placed on the plank, feet to the water. After the burial ceremony the plank is lifted at one end and the body slides into the sea. You can see the body go slanting down for a long distance.

Besides having storms, we had calms which lasted from two to five days at a time. Sometimes we had drifted forty or fifty miles out of our course. We did not have favorable winds. All the winds were head winds. . . . During the calm

the emigrants had a good time play-ing on deck, climbing up the riggings, dancing and playing games. One game we played all the time; that was pumping water out of the vessel, about ten men at a time on the pump. One of them would sing all the time making up the song as he pumped. Some of the words of the song were good and some ridicu-lous, but it helped to break the monotony.

I remember on one of the calm days the ship lay in the water rolling from side to side, and a porpoise, a fish from four to six feet in length and as fat as a pig, was playing about the ship, and the water [was] like a sheet of glass. Myself and some of the other young men started to climb the rigging. We chose the middle mast because it was the highest. We had climbed about half way up and the sailors thought they would have some fun by catching us up in the rigging and tying us up to the mast. They caught one boy on the first landing and tied him there. By this time I was at the top of the mast having a good time, and a boy named Kent was waiting for me to come down so he could climb to the top.

The sailors thought to catch me and tie me. Now up in the rigging there is not standing room for two so they stayed at the third landing from the top and let the Kent boy go down so they could catch me and tie me. About sixteen feet from the top is a guy rope[*] that runs down to the side of the ship deck to hold the mast steady. Instead of coming down the mast to where the sailors were, I swung on to the guy rope and slid down to the deck. The rope had been lightly tarred and was not dry and I was skinned and covered with tar from my ankles to my thighs. The sailors said I would have full run of the ship from that time on and so I was quite a favorite among them.

Things went along in about the same old style. Head winds and calms and we got short of fresh water and were put on half rations. But at last, after eight weeks and three days on the ship, we landed at New York. Stayed there two days and got on board the train.

Ebenezer crossed the Plains in a freight train, where he was employed as a cook. Later he was asked to serve as an "out-and-back rider," taking supplies to other companies as they crossed the Plains to the Salt Lake Valley. Ebenezer's parents and siblings left England and crossed the Plains a year after he emigrated. His father was buried along the Mormon Trail. Ebenezer married Mary Catherine Bullock and Veta Josephine Fjeldsted. Mary had five children and Veta had nine. He spent most of his life in Logan, Utah, where he was a butcher. He died February 13, 1920. His grandson was Harold Silver, who invented agricultural and mining machinery used throughout the world.

SOURCE: Farnes, Ebenezer. Reminiscences, 1–3. Typescript. LDS Church Archives. See also The Story of Ann Isacke Farnes and Her Family, compiled by Marilyn Austin Smith and Glenna King Austin. Typescript, 1972, in possession of family.

[*]
  A rope used to steady an object that is being hoisted or lowered

Mary Powell (Sabin)

"I grew to love the ocean."

BORN: November 6, 1842, Llanover, Monmouthshire, South Wales
PARENTS: John and Sarah Elizabeth Harris Powell
SAILING DATE: March 23, 1856
SHIP: *Enoch Train*
AGE: 13

efore leaving Wales we visited our relatives and bade them a fond
goodbye. We also visited among the Saints. They, of course, rejoiced
with us in that we were leaving for Zion.

I shall never forget the morning we took the train for Liverpool. Saints
from Abigaveni took us up to the station in an omnibus. A host of loving friends
were at the station to see us off.

After one week's stay in Liverpool we went on board the large American sail
boat, the *Enoch Train*. There were five hundred and thirty seven Saints in our
company. The ship's crew numbered thirty. On ship-board there was singing
and laughter and loud jesting among the crew. Somehow the excitement

In 1856, the Enoch Train *carried over 500 Saints to Zion.*

We were on the ocean seven weeks after we left Liverpool, England. The drinking water was bad and we couldn't drink it without boiling it. The "hardtack" we had to eat was eight or ten inches across. With the hardtack, bacon was served on our menu. The bacon was usually thick and fat and poorly cooked. Before sailing, mother toasted a quantity of bread, very dry and put it in a sack. We enjoyed this bread while it lasted.

—*Thomas Henry White emigrated at age 16, in 1863, aboard the* Antarctic.

seemed to turn me sick. Father said I was white as a sheet. The captain of the vessel stopped to talk to father. "You had better take your little girl down below," he said. They gave me a dose of medicine. . . . It put me to sleep. About midnight I awoke and lay observing my new surroundings. A large light shown in the arch way. My two sisters were sleeping peacefully beside me in the berth.

How strange to find ourselves out in the big ocean [the] next morning. Some members of the ship's crew were at work cleaning the floor of the boat. I took notice of their method, first scraping, next sweeping, then mopping. In this manner they cleaned the floor.

There was a stove on the boat called, "The Passenger Cook Stove." Upon it the passengers were allowed to cook things, each in turn. In order to make mother a [drink], father took up a kettle to the passenger cook stove. He put his name on it, John Powell. From time to time, all day long, I was sent to ask the cook, "Will you please tell me if John Powell's kettle is boiling?" Toward late afternoon, I met a couple of Scotsmen who laughed uproariously at my question. I ran back, and told father that he would have to fetch it himself. It took until five o'clock to get that cup for mother. After this experience, Father made arrangements with the captain's cook to boil the water on his stove [and] we no longer had to await our turn at

Julia Boline Mariane Clausen and an unidentified child of Odense, Denmark

the passenger's cook stove. Father [also] paid the captain's cook to prepare our food. [But] truth to tell, we ate little, due to seasickness.

There was a baby born on the ship. His parents named him Enoch Train, after the boat. It was the captain who suggested the name. My little brother was two weeks old when we commenced the voyage. We had named him while on the journey. After the christening, the captain came and gave him a souvenir, five dollars. But mother said, "No, the souvenir is for the baby that was born on the boat. Give it to him." So the captain gave the souvenir to little Enoch Train. . . .

Funny things to amuse us children happened every day. Once we watched two old men set their table and lay out their lunch, in careful, painstaking fashion. They asked the blessing on

Sometimes we had trouble cooking such things as rice and beans, which absorb so much water that we would not have sufficient to finish cooking them properly. This cooking was done on a sheet-iron stove about the size of an ordinary kitchen table, in a small room not much larger than a pantry. Many would be cooking at the same time, and would have to stand and watch their own things lest someone should come and push them back to give their own a better place.

The ship furnished a cook to attend to the fires and superintend things and assist the passengers. Father, having learned to cook at home when a boy and considering the galley, where the cooking was done, an unfit place for women, did our cooking himself.

—*Mary Lois Walker Morris emigrated at age 14, in 1850, aboard the* Josiah Bradley.

As far as I remember we were 50 days on the ocean. . . . The [drinking] water got to stink very much. I had to do some cooking for about 8 persons. I was most of the time sick. By standing before the hot stove stirring the rice which, however, got burned, the kitchen was always crowded by the folks. . . . I ate very little on board the ship. Our main food was salty pork, rice, and some potatoes. No bread but some hard crackers without salt. I did nearly starve and was very sick.

—*Gottlieb Ence emigrated at age 20, in 1860, aboard the* William Tapscott.

the food [and] just then a large wave came up and threw the dishes right and left. Everybody laughed, even the two old men. They had to scramble under the benches and in the far corners to pick up their cups and saucers.

One day father sent me to the "captain's galley" (or kitchen) to get some warm bread. I had to hurry back, for I had three [children] younger than I to watch and tend. I could not let them remain out of my sight many minutes.

I grew to love the ocean. Each afternoon I watched the sun sink like a ball of fire beneath the waves. Next morning it rose again out of the water. One day I stood looking over the banister on deck, [and] a sailor came and grabbed me saying, "Why are you leaning out so far?" "I want to see the ship plowing the waves and cutting the water," said I. He held me over the banister and I took a good look.

A good many people on the boat looked to father for numerous little favors. One man, seeing [him] always busy doing for others said, "Are you the captain?" "No," said father, "I'm just the chore boy." One day mother sent me on an errand to the upper deck. I ran along hand in hand with Ann Jones. The sea was very rough. I slipped and fell down, and pulled Ann down. In falling we bumped into an old sailor and I knocked him down. There we lay, all in a heap. Later we found that this old sailor had very poor eyesight, in fact, he was almost blind. Said he, "I have been on the ocean almost thirty years. This is the first time any girls have knocked me down."

One man said to Mother, "Sister Powell, your religion must go very deep to undertake a ocean voyage with so young a babe." He very kindly offered to supply some canned milk for the baby. "How much is it per can?" asked Mother. "Take it, to make us friends," he said.

When we had been on the ocean three weeks, Mrs. Deveroe [Devereux] died. They sewed her up in a sheet and buried her in the sea. [At] the commencement of the voyage, she remarked to my mother, "I'll go on board the ship and start my husband to Utah. If I should die, he will journey on. If we do not commence the journey, perhaps my husband and children will not reach Utah."

We had Sunday meetings on deck. There was a band that used to play each Sunday after meeting. Each night and morning, Saints assembled in the big room for prayers. We had a good time sailing, [and] everybody was congenial, pleasant and kind. [But] to be exact, the ocean voyage really did get tiresome at times, although we tried to make the best of it. We were on the ship five weeks and five days. Brother Ellsworth and Brother McAllister slept right across from our berth. They were full of fun and helped keep us lively.

One afternoon when the children were playing up on deck, I said, "Oh dear, I wish we'd soon reach land." Just then the captain held up his glasses and looked afar. I heard him whisper something about land to another man. I kept looking at a tiny speck ahead that seemed to increase. That night we passed a lighthouse. None of us children wanted to go below. We coaxed to be allowed to remain on deck just a little longer. At last the captain said, "All children below." We did not want to go down, [but] said

I was not seasick but the skipper showered me with so many nuts and raisins that I have never been able to eat them since.
—*Thomas Quayle emigrated at age 5, in 1841, aboard the Rochester.*

he, "I promise you tomorrow you'll see something much grander than a light-house."

Next morning we beheld two large hospitals situated in a beautiful green field. We did not go ashore for two days as we had to be examined first. Five hundred and twenty seven persons in all. Not one of our company was sent to either hospital. One was a general hospital and the other a mental hospital. The physicians declared that they had never seen a more healthy, cleanly company of immigrants. All this took place several miles from Boston.

We remained in Boston Harbor one day. While there a number of ministers came on board the *Enoch Train*. They distributed pretty picture cards among us children. Some building contractors came aboard and offered Father mason work at eight dollars per day. Father did not take the work. All the immigrants from the *Enoch Train* now traveled in a body to New York. We went by rail and water. At New York, Apostle John Taylor came to the boat and talked to the Saints. He impressed us very much standing there so erect and tall. I noticed his long beard. He was ready to address us [but] then he turned to the captain and said, "How long since these folks had any refreshments?" "Two days," was the answer. "Brethren and Sisters," said John Taylor, "I should like to see you eat before I speak to you." In less than half an hour, baker's bread, steak and [drinks] were brought onto the ship. I had not thought about being so hungry until then. How nice this food tasted.

[Then] Apostle Taylor spoke to the Saints and asked God to bless us with a safe journey to Utah.

Mary and her family eventually made their way to Iowa City, Iowa, where they joined the Church's first handcart company, led by Captain Edmund Ellsworth. They arrived in the Salt Lake Valley September 26, 1856. Unfortunately, her father died just two weeks after their arrival in Utah.

Mary married David Dorwart Sabin in 1864, and they became the parents of nine children. They lived in Payson and Salem, Utah. They ran a sawmill and a molasses mill. Mary's grandchildren remember her singing Welsh songs to them and baking wonderful cookies. Mary was widowed at an early age and boarded female school teachers to help provide for her family. It was one of those schoolteachers, Minnie Iverson Hoddap, who influenced Mary to record her remarkable personal history.

SOURCE: *Sabin, Mary. Autobiography, 5–8. Typescript. LDS Church Archives.*

PART THREE

Dangers and Deliverance

"Have I not commanded thee? Be strong and of a good courage;
be not afraid, neither be thou dismayed: for the Lord thy God is
with thee whithersoever thou goest."
—Joshua 1:9

Crossing an ocean between 1840 and 1890 was no small undertaking. Nearly seven hundred Latter-day Saints lost their lives while sailing to Zion between 1847 and 1869 alone. Their earthly remains were left in a watery grave. Many of those who died were children and elderly people—those least able to fight off the diseases that infested the living quarters of many seagoing vessels.

Infants and children were at greatest risk to the ravages of dehydration—the result of days and weeks of seasickness. Epidemics of measles, chicken pox, and other ailments took their toll, with numerous passengers being buried at sea.

Emigrants encountered terrifying storms, fog, near-collisions with icebergs, sharks following their ships, overcrowding below the main deck, cruel captains and sailors, and stale and wormy food. One little girl was so frightened by the violent rolling and pitching of the ship during a storm that she seemed to lose her sanity. She died two days later, having suffered from claustrophobia and sheer fright.

How were young Latter-day Saints able to endure the hard times? The stories that follow suggest that their courage came from at least two sources: first, from their absolute conviction of the truth of the restoration of the gospel of Jesus Christ and their belief that it was the will of the Lord that they gather with their fellow Latter-day Saints in the American West; and second, from the sustaining power of the love, support, and example of their fellow Saints. As seventeen-year-old Jacob Zollinger wrote, "We left for the gospel's sake and we had faith in the Lord." They needed faith and one another to make the journey. Once aboard the sailing ship or steamer, there was no turning back.

William Howard Anthony

"Willie my boy, where are you?"

BORN: August 10, 1860, Glasgow, Scotland
PARENTS: David and Agnes Young Anthony
SAILING DATE: July 14, 1868 [?]
SHIP: *Colorado* [?]
AGE: 7–8

During my childhood we resided in Glasgow, Renfrew, and vicinity. It was while we were at Renfrew, at Grandma's, when I was about three years old, that I nearly set the house afire. Grandmother had just died, and it must have been the winter season for the body was placed on an improvised bier [table] in front of and very near the large fireplace. I remember I was running around the room . . . and in my journeyings I had found a large ball of grease. Creeping under the bier, I placed it on the live coals in the fireplace. In a moment, and with a roar like thunder, a great blaze filled the fireplace. Just then a gust of wind came down the chimney and that blaze flew out nearly into the center of the room, enveloping the bier on which the

body of my grandmother lay. The folks in the other room heard the noise and oh, how excited they were! Buckets full of water were poured on the fire until it was extinguished but not before the sheet [wrapped around my grandmother's body] was badly scorched. Knowing my guilt, all that time I was hiding. But when the room was tidied up again and I was finally discovered, I did not get the whipping I deserved.

One night, in a dense fog, our ship struck a monstrous iceberg and was nearly wrecked, but was miraculously saved. It was a fearful experience. Everything that was not lashed down tight was thrown from side to side— people, utensils and luggage in one great pile. The rattle of pans, dishes and baggage, and the cries of women and children, the shouts of men, the commands of officers, the banging and bumping of the ship against the iceberg made it seem as if two monsters were trying to beat each other to pieces and the great floating mountain of ice would over- whelm the sturdy ship and sink her in the deep sea with all on board. But it was not to be so, we were in the hands of the "master of ocean and earth and skies."

—*Christopher Alston emi- grated at age 10, in 1864, aboard the* General McClellan.

When William's youger brother was about two years old, another brother was born named James. He lived only about six months. Shortly after this, William's parents divorced.

Mother's sister and her husband were in the United States and wanted us to emigrate and make our home with them. We boarded a coast- wise steamer and went to Liverpool. There we disembarked and took a transatlantic liner for the ocean voyage. I think it was the *Colorado.* As soon as we were under way, I began to wonder what was making the ship go. I thought I could find out if I looked over the side of the vessel, but my mother would not let me. When we walked the deck it was with my hand in hers. I puzzled over the motive power of that ship for a long time. At length I concluded that there must be something down in the water in front that was pulling it, but still Mother would not let me investigate.

One bright moonlit night, when Mother and Bob were fast asleep, I sneaked out of bed and went on deck in my nightgown. The moon was full and about four hours above the west horizon. Like a ghost, I sped to the front of the vessel; but leaning over as far as I could, the point where the ship struck the water was [still] invisible. Then I saw a pole about ten inches in diameter that extended from the front [of the ship] out over the water at about a thirty degree angle. I thought if I were out on that I could see under the steamer. I mounted the pole

and worked myself forward until I was about ten feet from the body of the ship.

There for the first time in my adventure, fear struck me, so I lay down on the pole and reached my arms and legs around it as far as they could go. I was in a precarious position. If I dropped it would be into the Atlantic Ocean, which was probably more than a mile deep, and be whirled under that mighty steamer. I could not turn around and I was afraid to creep [back toward] the ship, going backward. All this while the vessel plunged forward with awful speed, and at the same time swung from side to side like a mighty pendulum.

I was getting the greatest shock of my nine years of life and was beginning to think I could not hold on much longer when I heard a commotion on deck and Mother's voice saying, "Willie my boy, where are you?" I could not answer. At length a sailor spied me on my perch. He said, "Hang on little boy, don't try to come back. I will get you in a minute." He walked on that pole right out to me. I don't know how he did it, but I think there must have been a rope

We had one quite hard storm that shook things up some, but no great damage was done. Of course, the ship was being tossed about and was lurching badly. Two women right close to us were very much excited and crying. I could not help smiling although I had to keep a hold of the bunk to keep from being thrown out. I thought it absurd to suppose that a ship with 700 Saints bound for Zion could possibly sink. I, even then as a boy, . . . had faith we would be preserved, which we were and all except one man and child that died and were buried at sea came safely to land at New York on the 4th of June.

—*William Lindsay emigrated at age 12, in 1862, aboard the* John J. Boyd.

Some cattle that we had on board that were intended for beef were killed by the rolling and pitching of the vessel [and] were buried at sea, I well remember they were hoisted by block and tackle, swung over the ship's side, then dumped in the sea—food for sharks. I have heard it often said that sharks will follow a vessel for days if there is going to be a death, either man or beast.

—James Horrace Skinner was nearly 4 years old, in 1846, when he traveled on the Brooklyn *from New York to San Francisco.*

above his head he was holding to. When he got a good hold of the nape of my nightgown he pulled me to my feet and after he had shaken me said, "You little son-of-a-gun," only the word he said was much worse than "gun." In a few minutes I was in Mother's arms and that awful adventure was over.

We had a successful trip across the ocean and landed at Castle Garden, New York, about the last of August, 1868. While looking around in the new world, we spied a fruit stand. Mother said, "Look at those American apples, aren't they pretty?" She bought a big one and divided it, giving each a third. We took a bite and that was enough. We threw it away. It was years after that before I could eat a tomato.

We [boarded a train] at Castle Garden for Ogden, Utah, crossed the Plains without an unusual incident, and arrived in Ogden early in September. Aunt Janet and the hired man were there to meet us. They had a linchpin wagon, a part of which was a high box with two spring seats on it, as a means of conveyance. We mounted this vehicle, started an eighteen mile journey in a northerly direction and arrived at Three Mile Creek, where uncle's farm was located, that same evening. The threshers were there, so a feast was prepared for us and we settled down well pleased with the change from the old to the new world.

William Anthony married Jane Ann Young on October 28, 1879, and they became the parents of thirteen children. In his early years, he worked for the Denver and Rio Grande Railroad Company. However, he was severely injured in a gun accident

Icebergs at sea

and was thereafter unable to perform hard physical labor. He was a noted school teacher for thirty years and was also a deputy district assessor, a county treasurer, and a justice of the peace. He moved several times, living in Perry, Utah; St. John, Idaho; Portage, Utah; and Kimball, Idaho. He died September 1, 1940, in Blackfoot, Idaho.

SOURCE: *"Life History of William Howard Anthony." Typescript, in possession of Vernon Anthony, Firth, Idaho. See also Anthony, William. Autobiography.* In Our Pioneer Heritage, *compiled by Kate B. Carter, 12:87–88. Salt Lake City: Daughters of Utah Pioneers, 1969. The two narratives have been combined here.*

When we were sailing through the banks of Newfoundland we were in a dense fog for several days. The sailors were kept night and days ringing bells and blowing fog horns.

One day I was on deck with my father when I saw a mountain of ice in the sea, close to the ship. I said, "Look, father, look." He went as white as a ghost and said, "Oh my girl," at that moment the fog parted and the sun shone brightly till the ship was out of danger, when the fog closed on us again.

—*Mary Goble Pay emigrated at age 13, in 1856, aboard the* Horizon.

Ingre Marie (Mary) Larsen (Ahlstrom)

"On Christmas Eve the ship was struck by a hurricane."

BORN: August 21, 1836, Holdensgaard, Hjorring, Denmark
PARENTS: Christen and Johanna Marie Christiansen Larsen
SAILING DATE: December 12, 1855
SHIP: *John J. Boyd*
AGE: 19

I entered school at the age of seven, walking several miles to the village of Vaarsaa, which stood by the sea. The schoolmaster was a stern, dignified man, who tolerated no levity. I was being constantly impressed with the serious aspect of life. Our chief book of learning was the Bible. I learned to read fluently and having a tenacious memory, I had practically memorized the Bible before my twelfth year. My parents were Lutherans and at the age of fourteen I was confirmed into that church.

When I was eighteen, my parents were converted to a new religion which was brought to their door by two traveling missionaries, representing The Church of Jesus Christ of Latter-day Saints, commonly called the Mormons.

The terrors of a storm at sea

The principles of Mormonism were explained with such clarity and power, substantiated by so much Bible evidence that our family soon became converts. My parents and myself were baptized by immersion into the Mormon church on April 6, 1854.

One of the doctrines of the Mormon belief is the assembling together in the land of Zion, of the people of Israel from the nations of the earth. In order to obey this principle, it was necessary for us to dispose of all our belongings and travel over sea and land to far-away Utah, in the United States of America. Our friends and kindred did all in their power to dissuade us [from] what seemed to them a foolish credulity.

Despite their pleadings we left our beloved home in October, 1855. The family consisted of father, mother and eight children, the youngest a babe under two months of age. Our first stop was at Aalborg which had been appointed a temporary gathering place for Mormon converts. We camped in a large unfurnished hall where we made our beds on the floor and bought our food in the shops. Unfortunately an epidemic of measles broke out in the crowded camp. Many of the children became severely ill and with the arduous journey just ahead the epidemic became a source of great anxiety. When instructions came for us to proceed to Copenhagen, we bundled up the ailing children and took them with us. We had a rough crossing over the North Sea to England and suffered much from sea sickness.

The second and third decks were lighted day and night by large lamps suspended from the ceiling by chains. This allowed for the movement of the boat. Every day a man came [and] cleaned and refilled the lamps. One day while cleaning them, he spilt some coal oil on the steps. A lamp toppled over and immediately the whole stairway was ablaze. Father and others rushed to help and it was quickly put out before any damage was done.
—*Agnes C. Hefferan Richardson emigrated at age 7, in 1865, aboard the* Belle Wood.

We were both tired and hungry when we got to Liverpool. There they had a dinner for the company, some kind of soup. There were little bits of meat in it and lots of potatoes but it was so strong of pepper, ginger and salt I could not eat it. Here we were left in a large hall for one week and we were glad for that for we could go into town and buy all kinds of food ready to eat. We got good soup, meat and potatoes, rice, milk and anything we liked until we had everything ready [for the voyage].

It was the 12th day of December, 1855, when our ship was towed out of the Liverpool harbor, loaded with fresh water and provisions for the long voyage. There were five hundred and twelve Mormon converts aboard when we started, but the death rate was high especially among the children who had been weakened by the measles.

We had bad weather and heavy seas right from the first. On Christmas Eve the ship was struck by a hurricane and for a time it seemed that the old windjammer was doomed to be swallowed up in the sea. The storm raged so furiously that the luggage chests which were tied to posts on the deck, broke from their moorings and were hurled about with such force as to endanger life and limbs. All passengers were therefore ordered into their bunks where we crouched in misery, listening to the shrieking of the winds and wishing we were back in our comfortable homes again.

Sometime in January our ship caught fire on the first deck and [burned] through [to the second deck and filled it with smoke so that we nearly strangled. [Many passengers] ran up and

Hauling a shark on deck

Sunday, 25 March [1849], calm and hot, thermometer 117. A shark was caught and hauled on deck, which caused a lively scattering among the passengers.

—*Thomas Atkin emigrated at age 16, in January 1849, aboard the* Zetland.

wanted to jump overboard. Our leader, Canute Petersen said, "Stay on the ship. We will get the fire out and the ship will get to New York." And it did.

A few nights later we had a collision with another ship that almost knocked a hole in our ship. Our Captain had always been very cruel to the sailors. Now he flogged them worse than before, claiming the collision had been due to the crew's negligence.

On February 2, we saw a ship drifting helplessly before the wind. We steered toward it for four days before we were able to reach it and

Jacob Zollinger

A terrific storm came up while we were at sea. The storm lasted three days and three nights and it was impossible for anyone to walk on the deck and the children on board had to be tied in their berths to keep them in, the sea was terribly rough. During the storm the kitchens were broken in splinters and caught fire. The second time the fire broke out in the kitchens, they were so badly damaged that it was impossible for the passengers to cook in them. Two children died and were buried at sea.

—*Jacob Zollinger emigrated at age 17, in 1862, aboard the Windermere.*

rescue the thirty six sailors who were clinging to the rigging. They were a great help in sailing our ship as most of our own men were too badly disabled to work.

About this time, two of my little brothers died and were buried at sea. That was a severe blow to my mother. She never seemed to be the same after that.

I can imagine nothing more dreary than was our existence during that voyage on the *John J. Boyd.* But it came to an end at last and we landed in New York, February 16, 1856, having been sixty-six days in crossing the Atlantic from Liverpool, England.

The Larsen family traveled by train to the Mississippi River, then walked to Burlington, Iowa, where they worked to earn enough money to proceed to the Salt Lake Valley. While in Iowa, Mary married Jons Peter Ahlstrom, a Swedish convert to the Church. They came to the Salt Lake Valley in 1859 and were immediately asked by President Brigham Young to settle in Fort Ephraim in Sanpete County. They became the parents of nine children. Jons Peter made furniture and helped build the St. George and Manti temples. Mary enjoyed doing genealogical research and temple work for her Danish ancestors. Mary died on July 22, 1924, in Kanosh, Utah, and was buried near the temple in Manti. She was eighty-seven years old.

SOURCE: *History of Mary Larsen Ahlstrom. Typescript, 1–3, made available by Paul Ahlstrom Sr., Idaho Falls, Idaho. And also Ahlstrom, Mary Larsen. Autobiographical sketch, 1. LDS Church Archives. The two narratives have been combined here.*

Jay LeRoy Chatterley, Clifton Lunt Chatterley, John Chatterley,
and Earl Whittaker Chatterley

John Chatterley

"My cousin would play his fiddle, and I played my flute while the
sailors danced, and we had pretty lively times."

BORN: July 4, 1835, Salford, Lancashire, England
PARENTS: Joseph and Nancy Morton Chatterley
SAILING DATE: September 4, 1850
SHIP: *North Atlantic*
AGE: 15

On the morning that we sailed from Liverpool, my father had [my cousin] James [Morton] Thorpe and myself take the dogs on a walk, (two shepherds that we were bringing to Utah). As it would be the [last] chance for them to have a good run, as they were required to be chained up on board ship most of the time. We got to the dock just as the ship was leaving. It was about 10 or 13 feet from the edge of the dock, so we had to hire a boat to get on board the ship. The boatmen dallied and lingered until we got [out to] where the sea was rolling. The dogs had to be hauled up on deck,

We had not been on our way but a few days when our ship met with an accident. I think another ship ran into us, but we were near the Coast of Wales, and our captain turned around and went into Cardigan Bay, and I well remember my dear father being put over the side of the ship, on a plank with ropes and working on the damaged part of the ship. In a few days the repairs were completed and we started on our journey again.

—*Elizabeth Grace McCune emigrated at age 7, in 1851, aboard the* Ellen.

my cousin and myself had to climb up a ladder, and the boatmen charged three guineas, about 15 dollars.

The night before the ship sailed, and also the first night out, the captain let [the passengers] use the quarter deck for dancing. The weather was fine as we sailed down the River Mersey. When we got into the Irish Channel, it happened to be a little rougher than usual. We had very rough weather the second day out of Liverpool. The hatches had to be put on to keep the waves from splashing down in the steerage, where the passengers were. And, as the passengers had not secured boxes, bottles, and many other things as they had been instructed to do, the steerage floor was nearly covered with things, and it needed care and caution to get about. It was quite a sight to see the passengers, those that had courage to get up. Most were in their bunks sick,

Scandinavian women before their voyage to America

some praying, some hollering, wishing they were back home. [There were] all kinds of noises. . . .

There were only five passengers that could be on deck that day, my father, a man that had been a steward, an East India man, a man who had been a sheepherder in Australia, [and] a stowaway—an old sailor who had hid himself before the ship started. We were running to the cook's galley for [drinks] for the passengers until [long] into the night. I could hardly walk when we quit. [I] never was more tired in my life. I was not seasick one

minute nor were any of those that helped the passengers that day. It was a tough job serving the passengers as there were scores of cans, boxes, jugs, and all kind of things rolling about as the ship rocked about. It was hard work to keep on our feet. The sailors took quite a liking to me for what I did that day, being the only boy that was bold enough to come on deck.

When we got into the Atlantic ocean my cousin James Thorpe and myself had a good time with the sailors. My cousin would play his fiddle, and I played my flute while the sailors danced, and we had pretty lively times.

I got acquainted with a boy [the] same age as myself named Thomas Dallen [Dallin]. His folks settled at Springville, Utah. We [played] sport every day, and many times in the night. The sailors put us to painting some of the passengers with whiskers and mustaches as they slept on deck during the time we were near the equator. It caused lots of fun, and we didn't get found out, as we were decorated with the whiskers and mustaches ourselves.

In crossing the ocean we had a pretty stormy voyage until we got near the West India Islands, Cuba, Jamaica, San Domingo and others. The sea was rough, so that one of the main beams of the ship broke. When it snapped one of the sailors

It was fine in the morning. I saw 4 large fishes. The seamen said they [were] sea pigs. Their bodies looked very much like pigs. They would be about 60 stones each in weight.

—*George Wright emigrated at age 18, in 1860, aboard the* Underwriter.

When we reached what was called Devil's Pass we encountered a storm. This Devil's Pass is a place where if a boat gets too near [it] will whirl it about and very few ever get out of it again. In this storm the boat drifted over into Devil's Pass and about two in the afternoon the sailors began to holler "down deck, down deck" meaning for everyone to go down to the lower deck. It was terrible and water was coming in through the portholes and everything was slipping and sliding all over the deck.

Mother put us children up in a top bunk with a lot of Danish children. That is with the exception of my half-sister who couldn't be found again. When mother did find her she was up on top of a lot of baggage where one of the men had put her to be out of the water on the deck. Mother sat by the bed until about four o'clock in the morning so as to watch and care for us children. After the storm was all over and we were out of the Devil's Pass the captain said if it hadn't been for the Saints on board nothing could have saved us. There had never been a ship go down [in the Atlantic Ocean] that had any Saints on it.

—Emma Palmer Manfull emigrated at age 8, in 1874, aboard the Idaho.

hollered "There goes the main mast!" It was afterwards strengthened with a heavy bar of iron.

The Saints were organized into small companies and one from each company [was] appointed to get provisions, which consisted of hard crackers, pork, beans, molasses, vinegar, salt, oatmeal, and water. Most of the passengers had brought on board provisions that were more suitable and enjoyable than the ship's allowance. Meetings were held every Sunday and one night in the middle of each week. We had some excellent preachers on board. Captain Brown and sailors were very kind to the passengers. We arrived at New Orleans Nov. 1st, 1850. The captain and sailors said it was the stormiest voyage any of them had ever experienced.

Taking our sea voyage altogether we had a pretty good time. I was not sick a minute. Mother and James M. Thorpe were sick about 5 days.

[Sailing from New Orleans,] we arrived at St. Louis on the 8th of November on the steamer *Sultana.* The steamer *Sultana* was considered to be one of the finest steamboats that floated on the Mississippi River.

Previous to engaging the steamer the persons who had charge of the company of Latter-day Saints that came [across the ocean] in [our] ship [the] *North Atlantic,* were not aware that the steamer had 25 of her ribs broke, which happened on her last trip to New Orleans. Her captain, previous to making the trip, made a bet of one thousand dollars that he could carry as many bales of cotton as would load three sailing vessels of a certain size, and have some to spare. His steamer was loaded down until the main deck was under water, and bales of cotton were

Explosion of the steamboat Saluda, *on April 9, 1852—the most tragic river journey in Mormon history. At least 25 Latter-day Saints were killed in the accident, which took place near Lexington, Missouri.*

stacked so high that the steamer funnel could not be seen. Notwithstanding the bad condition of the steamer with her broken ribs, he raced [with another steamer] as we were traveling up the river, tying down the steam gauge and putting fat pine wood into the fire boxes, which made the steamer jump at every exhaust of the steam.

The president of the Saints remonstrated with him about his reckless conduct. It seemed that winning a few dollars was more important than the lives of his passengers and crew (over 500 people altogether). Our captain won his bet. A great many of the passengers would hardly sleep. They were afraid the boilers [might] burst, and according to some of the cabin passengers it was a very great risk.

Two years later, the side-wheel paddle steamboat Saluda *exploded with 175 passengers on board, including about 90 Latter-day Saints. The captain had ordered the steamboat to be pushed beyond its capacity. As a result, the boilers burst and a terrible disaster occurred—the worst in the history of navigation on the Missouri River.*

When we were in mid-ocean, I did a boyish prank. Outside, under the bow of the vessel, where [the] anchor and chains are hung, I ventured out unknown to my parents or anyone else. I sat there for some time and was able to see beneath a part of the vessel as the boat plowed through the ocean. This was a very dangerous thing for me to do. Had I slipped and fallen into the ocean, no one would have known what had become of me. But I climbed back safely.

—Olof Jenson emigrated at age 9, in 1866, aboard the Humboldt.

John Chatterley and his family crossed the Plains and arrived safely in the Salt Lake Valley in September of 1851. President Brigham Young called them to settle in Iron County, Utah. John married Sarah Whittaker March 12, 1862, and they became the parents of nine children. John was a prominent and respected citizen in Cedar City, Utah, where he was a schoolteacher, postmaster, mayor, and city recorder. He was the manager of a dramatic association and spent many hours in music and drama rehearsals, frequently held in the Chatterley home. He directed a brass band and a local community choir. The neighborhood children were always welcome at the Chatterley home, where they enjoyed playing on their swings, hammocks, teeter-totters, and whirligigs. John died May 2, 1922, in Cedar City, Utah.

SOURCE: *Chatterley, John. Autobiography.* Utah Pioneer Biographies, *7:68–72, 74. Family History Library. Ordering of paragraphs has been modified extensively to reflect chronological time.*

Peter Gottfredson (far left), his wife Alice (far right), and 12 of their 14 children

Peter Gottfredson

"A very rough voyage"

BORN: April 17, 1846, Sanderby, North Jutland, Denmark
PARENTS: Jens and Karen Jensen Gottfredson
SAILING DATE: December 12, 1855
SHIP: *John J. Boyd*
AGE: 9

Two Mormon missionaries, the future Apostle Erastus Snow and Christian Fjeldsted, converted and baptized Peter's parents in Denmark in 1851. The family endured much criticism and persecution because of their conversion.

I had several uncles, aunts, and cousins, and none of them were Mormons, but they were kind to [our family] which was not the case with all the people. The small boys picked at me, because my parents were Mormons. At one time they wanted me to swear like they did. My parents had told me it was wicked, and because I would not swear, they rolled

One day Father took me down into the third class which was the hold. There the conditions were really terrible. People packed in like cattle, about seven or eight hundred of them. The stench was terrible. This was all very shocking to Father.

—Agnes C. Hefferan Richardson emigrated at age 7, in 1865, aboard the Belle Wood.

me in high grass, when it was wet with dew, until I was as wet as if I had been dipped in water. We were on our way to school when the teacher asked what made me so wet, and I told him. He took the boys to task and they did not molest me any more. That incident may have had something to do with me not getting into the habit of profaning. I cannot remember ever taking an oath. I could not see any satisfaction in it.

Early in the month of December, 1855, we left Aalborg [Denmark] to go to America. We stayed in Copenhagen a few days visiting father's sister and her husband. From there we crossed the Baltic Sea to Kiel, and by rail to Gluckstadt. Thence by steamer to Grimsby, England and to Liverpool by rail and sailing from there on the 12th of December on the ship *John J. Boyd,* under the leadership of Knud Petersen who had filled a mission to Norway and Denmark. There were 508 passengers on board. Knud Petersen became president of Sanpete Stake of Zion. He was father-in-law of President Anthon H. Lund.

We had a very rough voyage over the Atlantic. We got to New York on the 16th of February, 1856, [having been] sixty-five days on the water. We had headwinds most of the way. When we were about one-third of the way over we were driven back to the coast of Ireland. The vessel was on fire twice. The one time was serious. The fire started in the Captain's cabin and burned through the deck and filled the vessel with smoke so that the passengers had to go on deck. Some trunks and other baggage that was on fire was thrown into the sea.

There was much sickness on board and I remember more than thirty deaths. I will here describe a funeral at sea. After the customary services the corpse was sewn into a canvas, or sheet, with a large lump of coal at the feet. A plank was laid over the side of the vessel and the corpse laid on it with feet out. A prayer was offered, the end of the plank raised and the dead slid into the sea, feet foremost, and all was over.

Several of the sailors were disabled and some died. The captain was very cruel to the sailors. At one time the vessel sprang a leak, water was running in fast. About thirty sailors were working a large double lever pump with ropes attached to the ends of the levers. One sailor was not working to suit the captain. He picked up a rope with a heavy hook in the end, and from behind hit the sailor on the head with the hook, killing him instantly. I stood nearby watching the pumping and saw it. So did some others. The ship was getting short of able-bodied sailors to man the ship and the captain planned to [draft] passengers to take the place of disabled sailors.

One morning I had occasion to go on deck very early, and looking ahead saw what I thought was a steamship. I went below and told the folks that we would soon be to land, that there was a steamship not far ahead. Some of the passengers went up on deck to see, and when the captain turned his [looking] glass on it, [he] discovered that it was a wrecked vessel. What I thought was a smoke stack was a stump of broken mast. Part of the

On May 10 [1864] a terrible storm arose and my father tied me to a timber with a rope to keep me from being hurled about by the pitching of the ship. An old uncle of mine had a big kettle of peas which he had cooked. He sat down to enjoy the dish. The next thing I saw was the old man sliding back and forth under his berth in these peas.

—*Martha Olson Sprague emigrated at age 10, in 1864, aboard the* Monarch of the Sea.

We had a rough day. We could scarcely walk about. The ship rocked so very much a very many fell down and spilled their soup and potatoes and cakes and pies. The tin bottles and boxes [were] rolling about and men and women falling down and sliding under the berths and crushing the bottles' sides together and hurting themselves at times.

—*George Wright emigrated at age 18, in 1860, aboard the Underwriter.*

bulwarks [on the wrecked vessel] had been torn away by the sea, and the waves had swept over the ship and one of the sailors had been swept overboard. Mutiny occurred on our ship. The captain did not want to rescue the sailors of the disabled ship. The mates did. We were told that the mates and the crew put the captain in confinement. The first mate, with two sailors, took a small boat and rowed to the disabled ship. The second mate took charge of the ship.

The sailors from the wrecked ship came to our ship in a large white boat that held all of them, as I remember thirty-five. They came to the side of our ship and a rope ladder was let down that they came up on. Their boat was hoisted on to our ship. Our mate and the two sailors were hoisted up in their boat. The wrecked ship was loaded with flour from America [to be delivered] to England. It was left to drift where it would. We watched it as long as we could see it.

At one time the captain said to Knud Peterson [Petersen], "If I hadn't [these] damned Mormons on board I would have been in New York six weeks ago. Peterson [Petersen] said to him, "If you hadn't Mormons on board, you would have been in hell six weeks ago."

Our drinking water got bad before we landed and the provisions gave out except some hard sea biscuits. Father had brought his Danish military uniform, sword, gun and bayonet which had been presented to him. They were sewed up in canvas. When we landed they could not be found. They had either been taken or lost. He wanted to keep them as relics. When we landed in New York it was said the captain was not on the ship. It was thought he had got away on a fishing or trading boat. . . .

Apostle John Taylor was at New York to look after the emigrants when they landed. He was very kind and attentive to [us]. We stayed there about a week. We learned that it was providential that we were so long on the sea, for when we got to New York the trains had been snow bound for a long time and could not run for several days after we landed and we would have been on expense. The ship company furnished the provisions as long as we were on board the ship. When we left New York the roads were yet in bad condition and we had to travel very, very slow. I remember in places the men would walk beside the train. Most of the immigrants hadn't enough means to take them through to Utah, and had to remain in the States. Some stopped in Illinois, some in Missouri and others in Iowa. We stayed in Alton, Illinois.

Father worked at a brick kiln at Alton, Illinois, at a dollar a day. He worked there till June when he and I took the chills and fever and was confined to our beds most of the time for a month, till after mother's death. Mother was afflicted with consumption [tuberculosis] and died on the 4th of July, 1856. It was called "weaver's consumption." She had woven on a hand loom most of her life and lint from the material was breathed into her lungs which caused irritation and the infection. Before leaving

Among the Saints were two English sailors of note. One was the late Francis Daily and the other was his friend. While in the iceberg district, seeing the anxiety on the face of the captain, they asked to be allowed to pilot the ship through the danger. They were permitted, and after the danger was passed they received the congratulations of all.
—*Louisa Harriett Mills Palmer emigrated at age 12, in 1862, aboard the* Manchester.

Denmark mother dreamed of the journey to America. She described crossing the ocean and getting to where she died. She did not dream of getting to Utah.

Shortly after mother's death we went to St. Louis, Missouri where we stayed about a year. . . . In the spring of 1857 we sailed up the Missouri River to Florence, Nebraska. We stayed there a short time until we started for Utah with Christian Christiansen's Handcart Company.

The Gottfredson family went with the handcart company only as far as Genoa, Nebraska, and then returned to Omaha to earn more money for the journey west. They eventually crossed the Plains in 1858 with a small company of Danish Latter-day Saints, composed of only six wagons, led by Ivor N. Iverson. Along the way, they traveled for some time alongside a group of soldiers from Johnston's Army, who were also on their way to Utah. The soldiers paid special attention to Peter, now twelve years old, who apparently was "the biggest boy in camp." They let him ride one of their mules and drive some of their livestock.

After the death of Peter's mother, his father married Karen Marie Pedersen Meilhede. The Gottfredson family eventually settled in Vermillion, Sevier County, Utah. Peter and his brother and sister played the violin for dances to earn money. Peter married Amelia Gledhill in 1872 in Salt Lake City, and they became the parents of ten children, the last of which was stillborn. Amelia died shortly thereafter.

After Amelia's death in 1893, Peter married Alice Adell Keeler, and they had five children. Peter was a bishop in Vermillion for twenty years. He served in the Blackhawk War for three years and spent several years compiling stories about the Indians and the early settlers. Using his own money, he published a book in 1919 called Indian Depredations in Utah, *a collection of histories, newspaper articles, and documents relating to the Blackhawk War. In Sevier County, Peter was elected justice of the peace and a selectman. He was interested in politics all his life. He was a beekeeper during his later years. He died February 20, 1934, in Richfield, Utah.*

SOURCE: Gottfredson, Peter. Autobiography, 1–11. Typescript. LDS Church Archives.

Gibson Condie

"I consider we were greatly blessed."

BORN: March 10, 1835, Clackmannan, Clackmannan, Scotland
PARENTS: Thomas and Helen Sharp Condie
SAILING DATE: January 29, 1849
SHIP: *Zetland*
AGE: 13

After boarding our ship the *Zetland*,] Brother Orson Pratt and [a] few other elders came on board the vessel, and organized us and appointed Brother Orson Spencer as our president with his two counselors, Brother James Ure and Brother Mitchell. Brother Pratt then stated to the Saints, "If you would follow the direction and advice of those brethren we have appointed all will be well with you." He also blessed the Saints and he gave them some good counsel and advice [on] how to be clean, and [that they] not forget their prayers, and [that if they lived] as Saints and respect the ship's officers all would be well with them. He promised them the ship would arrive in New Orleans with the Saints all safe.

[We had a storm] so terrific that one of our masts was split and wrapped with chains, and all the sails were taken down. The Captain became so discouraged over the unsatisfactory conditions that he forbid any of us to sing or pray on the vessel. But this did not prevent us from fasting and praying in secret which was ordered done by President [Knud] Peterson, after which better weather prevailed.

—Andrew Madsen emigrated at age 20, in 1855, aboard the John J. Boyd.

It was a time of rejoicing to the Saints to have an Apostle, Brother Pratt, giving us such good counsel and advice, filled with the Spirit of the Lord, promising us in the name of the Lord that all would be well with us and [that we would] arrive in safety. Also the beautiful hymns was sung for that occasion, farewell hymns, etc. Orders given to set up sail.

A steamer came along then and pulled us out of the docks into the Irish Channel. The Saints then took a last look of their native land. While many shed tears, parting with their friends and singing their farewell hymns, it was very touching almost to everyone.

When we was in the Irish Channel the steamer then returned back again to Liverpool, accompanied by several of the elders from Liverpool. Our ship was then left to herself. Then the ship began to toss to and fro. The buckets or cans would tip over. The people then began to be sick, dizzy, [and] began to vomit. They could not sit up nor eat anything. They call it seasickness.

Everyone [who] goes to sea generally [has] that attack, [which] lasts three days and sometimes longer. A person [does] not feel like eating. They feel as though they could not live. I was [seasick] about a week myself before I was able to be round again.

Shortly after we left the docks, the first mate of our vessel got drunk and neglected his duties while we were in the Irish Coast or Channel. It is [a] very dangerous sea full of rocks, &c. Our ship had a narrow escape from being dashed to pieces. She run against some rocks. The captain thought [there was] something wrong. He then saw for himself the danger of the vessel, and he took charge and changed the course of the vessel. He then took first mate into custody. He was not permitted to be on deck on daytime, only at night. His office was took from him. He was a prisoner all the way to New Orleans. The Lord was over us and preserved us from the jaws of death. [In] another circumstance, our galley (fireplace) got on fire. We were all frightened, our vessel being on fire [and] no way to escape [except] only to jump into the sea and be drowned. We succeeded in then checking the flames. We all felt thankful to our Heavenly Father [for] preserving us [in] the two narrow escapes we had. On Sundays the captain gave permission for the Saints to have their meetings on deck and it was well attended. Good order prevailed. Generally the captain and most of the crew would listen very attentively and come regular to our meetings. The Saints were well pleased with their president, Brother Spencer and they greatly respected the captain, always at his post if [there] were any danger.

We enjoyed ourselves pretty well on the ship. We would amuse ourselves [with] all kinds of games, [including] playing checkers. We would set our hook and line by the side of the ship [to] catch the fish. It was a grand sight to see the beautiful fishes of all kinds. They were very large.

Well, I took very sick on the boat. They thought for sure I was going to die. Mother had the doctor come down to see me. He told her to get me up on deck and let me stay there in the air. Sometimes the waves would get so high I could lie there and watch them.

Grandmother Johnson came up several times a day though and sat with me. She was awfully good to me on the boat and she made a little cloth bag that she hung around my neck and every day she filled it with cookies and dainties that she had brought with her from England. My sister and brothers came up every day to see me and they would eat the cookies and things and I was too sick to care. Grandmother Johnson would find them gone and she would tell mother she knew I was getting better because I [had] eaten all those things. Mother worried for fear I would die and they would have to bury me at sea. She would just sit and wring her hands when she thought of it. I think that would be an awful thing to have to bury one of your children in the ocean. I got well, however, and was able to survive the trip.

—*Ruth Blair Evans emigrated at age 7, in 1868, aboard the* Minnesota.

One day a terrible storm came up. I was standing on the middle of the deck holding to a large barrel just under the hold of the ship. I felt impressed to move under the deck and just as I did so, and had gone a short distance, a mast beam broke and fell, breaking the barrel to pieces. So you see how necessary it is to heed the promptings of the Spirit at all times.

—Annie Catherine Christensen Olsen emigrated at age 12, in 1855, aboard the James Nesmith.

There were many a day that I have been amused to see them play around the ship.

The sailors [also] set their hook and line hanging by the side of the ship. One day the sailors hauled up a dolphin on deck. It was a large fish, larger than a horse. We were scared to see this monster. The sailors cut it in pieces [and] gave [it] to the passengers; some would eat, others did not care about it.

If t[here] were any sickness on board we would see the sharks follow the ship for days. I think we lost two children [to] death on the voyage. They sew[ed] them up in a sheet and threw them overboard. The sharks then are ready to devour [them]. It is [a] very sad affair to throw the dead overboard to be devoured . . . by the sharks.

If [there] were any quarreling on ship it would be around the galley or fireplace on account of [passengers'] pots on the fire. They would remove [other people's] pots to one side; they then would put theirs [in their place]. They would get angry and have hard words one with another. While on ship, a man wished to be baptized. On his request it was granted to him.

It was a grand sight to see Jamaica Island. When we came in sight, the natives in their canoes would come along and bring different kinds of fruit to sell. They would get in our ship. I should think we [were] two miles from land, [and] we would then see other islands day after day. The largest of the islands is Cuba. The natives with their canoes would come for miles out to sea and sell fruits, fishes and nuts, etc.

I consider we were greatly blessed. [We] enjoyed health & strength, having good times on the ship, free from diseases. We were about nine weeks on ship. [After arriving at] New Orleans by steamer, [we bid] adieu the faithful ship *Zetland*, also the captain & officers.

After arriving in New Orleans, Gibson and his family made their way to Iowa. They bought land on Mosquito Creek, one and a half miles east of Kanesville (now Council Bluffs), where they lived for over two years, earning money for the rest of their journey west. There Gibson learned the trade of making wagons. He and his family crossed the Plains, arriving in Salt Lake City on September 2, 1852. Gibson wrote in his journal, "I am very thankful to my Heavenly Father for preserving us, and [to] be with the body of the Church in the valleys in the mountains."

Gibson helped dig the foundation for the Salt Lake Temple and was present at the ceremonies for the groundbreaking and laying of the cornerstone for the temple. He had many great trials. During the drought and grasshopper plague of 1855, Gibson lived mostly on roots, going hungry much of the time. He also suffered with frozen feet after helping to clear snowdrifts up to sixteen feet deep so rescue wagons could travel to meet the stranded handcart companies in 1856. In 1857 he met, courted, and married Elizabeth Robinson, a survivor of the Edward Martin Handcart Company. He and Elizabeth were sealed by President Brigham Young and became the parents of twelve children. Gibson lived a long and productive life, much of it in Croyden, Utah. He died on January 24, 1913, in Preston, Idaho. Gibson is an ancestor of Elder Spencer J. Condie of the Seventy.

SOURCE: Condie, Gibson. Reminiscences and diary, 23–25. Holograph. LDS Church Archives.

The Brooklyn *was a square rigger which brought about 234 Saints from New York to San Francisco in 1846.*

PART FOUR

Two Unique Voyages:
The *Brooklyn* (1846) and The *Julia Ann* (1855)

"We were so closely crowded that the heat of the Tropics was terrible,
but 'mid all our trials the object of our journey was never forgotten.
The living faith was there and was often manifested."
—*Caroline A. Perkins Joyce Jackson*

Every one of the voyages that carried Mormon immigrants to the United States between 1840 and 1890 was unique in some way. There would have been a voyage that had the worst food; one that endured the most frightening storms; and one that experienced the most burials at sea. There was probably even a voyage with the nicest captain; one with the cutest sailors; and one that was followed by the meanest-looking sharks. Though each voyage was unique in its own way, two special voyages are highlighted here: The *Brooklyn* and The *Julia Ann*. The 1846 voyage of the *Brooklyn* was the longest voyage to carry Latter-day Saints to their destination. It took six months! This voyage was also distinct because it carried Mormon immigrants from the East coast to the West coast. Most Latter-day Saint immigrants made this journey across the Plains, not by a sea voyage. The 1855 voyage of the *Julia Ann* was unique because of all the voyages that carried Latter-day Saint immigrants to America, it was the only one lost at sea.

The *Brooklyn* (1846)

On February 4, 1846, the same day the Mormon pioneers began leaving Nauvoo, Illinois, to cross the Plains in covered wagons, the ship *Brooklyn* sailed out of New York Harbor carrying 234 Latter-day Saints bound for San Francisco Bay. These Saints were among hundreds of new members of the Church living along the Atlantic seaboard who wanted very much to gather with the Saints in the West. Under the direction of Elder Samuel Brannan, passengers were recruited during the winter of 1845–46, and the ship was chartered to sail around South America's Cape Horn and then north to California.

Those aboard the *Brooklyn* included 70 men, 63 women, and 101 children—half of whom were under the age of six. Conditions aboard this ship were not particularly comfortable. The ship was not very big, and families lived between decks in a cramped area with low ceilings. Only the children could stand upright.

The voyage took a long time—six months. Most of the passengers experienced some seasickness. At one time a storm blew the *Brooklyn* almost to the Cape Verde Islands off the coast of Africa! When it finally sailed around Cape Horn, it was so cold that crew members had to be lowered down the sides of the ship to chip away ice. Food became stale and wormy. Drinking water became slimy and tasted terrible.

During the long voyage, the *Brooklyn* stopped for several days at the Juan Fernández Islands, about 400 miles west of Chile in the Pacific Ocean. There, they loaded up the ship with wonderful fresh fruits and vegetables, as well as 18,000 gallons of fresh drinking water. They washed their clothes and took much-needed baths. Traveling on to Hawaii, they dropped off a shipment of supplies before coming to California. They finally came ashore in what is now San Francisco Bay on Friday, July 31, 1846.

Many of the *Brooklyn* passengers worked in California to earn money to buy provisions to continue their journey to the Salt Lake Valley. Some of them were working at Sutter's Mill when gold was first discovered. Most of the Saints were not interested in the gold rush that followed and, instead, obeyed President Brigham Young's counsel to join the main body of the Church in the Salt Lake Valley.

The *Julia Ann* (1855)

Nearly 550 voyages carried Mormon immigrants to America between 1840 and 1890. Of these voyages, only one known ship was lost at sea: the *Julia Ann*.

In 1855, a small group of converts to The Church of Jesus Christ of Latter-day Saints set sail from Sydney, Australia, headed for California. Their ship, the three-masted *Julia Ann,* was loaded with 350 tons of coal and carried 56 passengers, including 28 Latter-day Saints. The voyage was expected to take about 80 days.

After 26 days at sea, however, the *Julia Ann* encountered a storm late one night in the Pacific Ocean (see picture on page 125). With a tremendous crash that sounded like thunder, the ship was blown head-on into a hidden coral reef near the Scilly Islands, 400 miles west of Tahiti. Two women and three children were drowned as the ship broke in half and eventually sank. The remaining passengers climbed onto the reef in waist-high cold water, where they waited and shivered until morning. They recovered a few supplies from the heavily damaged ship and were able to make it to a nearby island. They survived for two months by eating coconuts, crabs, and sea turtles.

The *Julia Ann* was a total loss, but Captain Benjamin Franklin Pond and nine crew members were able to repair a small life boat. Captain Pond and his crew rowed 250 miles against stiff trade winds to the island of Bora-Bora in French Polynesia for help. They sailed back aboard the schooner *Emma Packer* and found the castaways still on the Scilly Isles. John Eldredge, a returning missionary from Australia, wrote: "I need not attempt to describe our feelings of gratitude and praise which we felt to give the God of Israel for His goodness and mercy in His working a deliverance for us."

James Horace Skinner

"A long and tedious voyage of six months."

BORN: April 16, 1842, Warpole, New Hampshire
PARENTS: Horace Austin and Laura Ann Farnsworth Skinner
SAILING DATE: February 4, 1846
SHIP: *Brooklyn*
AGE: 3½

James H. Skinner was only six weeks shy of his fourth birthday when he sailed aboard the Brooklyn, *yet vivid memories of the six-month voyage remained with him throughout his life. James also recounts stories his parents told him in later years.*

In the month of February, 1846, we left our home, my native land and all our friends, with Father, Mother and a numerous lot of immigrants. We sailed [from New York Harbor] in the ship, *Brooklyn* for California. Our ship was a good, staunch, tub of a whaler, that had been changed from a whaler to an immigrant or passenger ship.

With few accommodations or conveniences, we were herded in like sheep in a pen, but we made the best of it that we could. This was to be our home for a long and tedious journey (voyage) around Cape Horn, the [southernmost] point of South America.

We suffered all the hardships of a sea voyage: . . . storms, close confinement, hardtack, sickness, heat, and sea-sickness. Before we reached Cape Horn, we encountered a terrible storm. The hatches were battened down, to keep the waves that ran mountain high from [flooding] down below, and swamping the ship. It seemed at times as if every minute would be our last. The ship was tumbling and rolling so, that it was impossible to stand, [except] by holding to something firm. While the tempests were raging above, we below were being tossed about like feathers in a sack.

While in this condition, the good old Captain came down among us, looking as though our last days had come. We tried to gather around him and heard him say, "My friends, there is a time in our lives when it is fitting to prepare to die. That time has come to us, for I have done all I can do. Unless God intercedes, we must go down." Someone answered and said, "Captain, we were sent to California, and we shall go there." He went back on deck, saying, "These people have a faith that I have not got." We outrode that storm in safety.

Ships docked at port

Burial at sea

Another terrible storm overtook us as we were rounding Cape Horn, but by
kind providence we passed through that, too, in safety, as we had a mission to
perform.

[One] remembrance was the burial at sea of a [person who] died on our
voyage to California. As I remember, the corpse was placed in a sheet or shroud,
then placed on a plank, one end resting on the side of the vessel, the other held
by supports. [I remember] the people standing around the corpse. After the
service was over, one end of the plank was raised enough to let the corpse
gently slide off and disappear into the mighty and lonesome ocean. My mother
[held] me tight in her arms as if in fear that I, too, might find a watery grave.

Some cattle that we had on board that was intended for beef were killed by
the rolling and pitching of the vessel were buried at sea. I well remember they
were hoisted by block and tackle, swung over the ship's side, then dumped in
the sea—food for the sharks. I have heard it often said that sharks will follow a

vessel for days if there is going to be a death, either man or beast.

My next recollection was when we landed at [the] Juan Fernández [Islands], where we stopped for water. This is—or was—the home of Alexander Selkerk [whose experiences gave Daniel Defoe the idea for his book *Robinson Crusoe*]. We visited the cave where it is said he made his home with his captive and companion, his man Friday, whom he captured from the cannibals.

A good sister (Laura) Goodwin, a very warm friend of our family, died and was buried on [one of the] San Juan Fernández Islands. She left seven children to be cared for. The Goodwin family and our people were always the best and closest of friends—more like brothers and sisters than just friends. Bro. Goodwin had a hard struggle for some time, with no wife and seven children to look after and care for. One of the boys—Albert—is my neighbor as I write this [in] 1915.

Our fare on shipboard was not of the best you can believe, consisting mostly of hard-tack and salt junk with now and then a change, as on Thursday [when] we had apple duff [a sweet doughy pudding boiled in a bag]. This was an extra treat to us. At times it was too rough to make even [apple] duff, but as mother expressed it, we were very happy, knowing that we were doing the will of the Lord, and that he would not forsake [us] in [our] hour of need. Her faith was always strong as long as she lived. She bore a strong testimony as she lay on her death bed.

We lay some three weeks becalmed under the burning tropical sun. Not a breeze. What air we had was [as] if it came out of a furnace. The sea

Temperance Westwood (Moon)

Temperance Westwood (Moon) came to America from England at the age of 9 aboard the *Ashland*. One day during the voyage, she was knocked down some steep stairs by two men carrying a trunk. The men had not seen her. She was hurt badly and bedridden for many days. The ship leaked constantly and sunk on its way back to Liverpool, England.

Henry Moon

Henry Moon was on the very first ship, the *Britannia,* that sailed from England carrying new Latter-day Saint converts. They left Liverpool June 6, 1840. Despite three storms and much sickness, all passengers reached America 41 days later, safe and happy.

was like molten glass. The Captain ordered an awning rigged up to protect the passengers from the excessive heat. There we would sit or lie, panting like lizards in Death Valley. At times, a breeze would spring up, perhaps a half a mile away, often further away. At times [a breeze] would strike us, and move the ship perhaps a few miles. How happy and refreshed would [we] poor mortals be, after [our] terrible suffering. It was so hot that the pitch was drawn out of the ships seams. Oh, how the people suffered. I [desire] the reader to imagine our suffering.

At last we reached our destination and haven of safety after a long and tedious voyage of six months, buffeted by wind and waves, thanking our Heavenly Father for His watchful care and mercy in bringing us safely through our many trials and dangers. We arrived in what is now known as San Francisco, California, (then known as Yerba Buena—meaning a good herb), on the last day of July, 1846, to find our country at war with Mexico.

[It was] a country barren and dreary, not like the California of today. As I remember, where San Francisco now stands it was covered with chaparral, manzanita, poison ivy, and mesquite, with very little fresh water.

Before we had time to get settled or anyway fixed to live, Father and Mr. Austin, with most of the men of our Company, were called to go up the Sacramento River to load the ship with Redwood, hides, and tallow for her return trip home to New York. While they were gone their families were to draw rations from the stock that was brought with them from home, but what they got was something scandelous, not enough to hardly keep life in their bodies. . . .

Soon after Father and Brother Austin left, mother and Sister Austin, with their families and with what food they could get, moved to the Mission Dolores, some three miles from San Francisco. To try and help make a living for themselves and [their] children, [they] opened a small eating house with what they had or could get in the way of food. . . . After the [Mexican women] got acquainted with them, and found that the Mormons were friends, not enemies, the [Mexican] women helped them what they could with milk, beef, chickens, eggs, onions, beans, etc. You must remember, the United States was at war with Mexico. We were right in the midst of war, but as providence would have it, there was peace around where we were, for which we were very thankful. . . .

My first schooling was in San Francisco. The first and only time I played hooky was here. In going back to school after [lunch] I ran across a man with a hand organ and a monkey. That afternoon I forgot all about school [and followed] the man and the monkey around.

The Skinner family moved to San Bernardino, California, in 1850 and then moved to Beaver, Beaver County, Utah, in 1858. As a young man, James herded cattle and horses and helped to build school houses, church houses, and homes. Later, he participated in the construction of the St. George Temple. He helped set up the Deseret Telegraph Line through the community, attended telegraphy school, and managed the local telegraph office. He served a mission to the New England States from 1876 to 1877. James married Ellen Cartwright August 1, 1860. They became the parents of thirteen children. James was in the furniture business for thirty years. He died March 28, 1917, in Beaver City, Utah.

SOURCE: *"History of James Horace Skinner, Utah Pioneer, 1842–1917," 1–7. Typescript, in possession of Rohn Susan Brown, Salt Lake City, Utah. See also "The Ship Brooklyn Saints." In* Our Pioneer Heritage, *compiled by Kate B. Carter, 3:579–81. Salt Lake City: Daughters of Utah Pioneers, 1960. Steven and Janet Soulier, of North Logan, Utah, also provided valuable third-person information on the Skinner family.*

Thought to be Peter Penfold

Peter Penfold

"She suddenly struck on a coral reef."

BORN: June 22, 1831, Lamberhurst, Kent, England
PARENTS: John and Elizabeth Thompson Penfold
SAILING DATE: September 7, 1855
SHIP: *Julia Ann*
AGE: 24

This letter was written by Peter from Tahiti to the Latter-day Saints in Australia. It was read in conference when word of the mishap was first announced to the Saints, and it was published in the Zion's Watchman, *the Australian Mission periodical, on May 24, 1856. Peter was the youngest passenger aboard the* Julia Ann *known to have written about that experience.*

Tahiti February 17th, 1856
Dear Brothers & Sisters,
I now take the present opportunity of writing you a few lines hoping

[to find] you all well. Since we left Australia we have passed through dangers, difficulties, hardships and trials.

We set sail as you are aware on the 7th of September [1855]. All went on pretty well until the 3rd [of] October. That evening about half past eight o-clock, when the winds was blowing free and the *Julia Ann* was going about 12 or 13 knots per hour, she suddenly struck on a coral reef off Scilly Island about 300 to 400 miles west of Tahiti and became a total wreck.

When she first struck, some of us was singing on the top of the midship house. We soon got down and went into the house, but finding that not very

Painting of the Julia Ann

safe we went into the cabin, the sea breaking over us every moment. It was a thing impossible to stand. A rope was soon conveyed to [some nearby] rocks.

Father, mother, Stephen and most of the men went on shore by [means of] the rope while I was down in the cabin lending assistance to the women and children that was still below and to help them up on the poop [a deck at the back of the ship]. Sister Humphries and Sister Harris and infant was drowned in the cabin. Little Mary Humphries and Marion Anderson was washed off the poop [deck] and drowned. They are all that was lost.

After I had helped get them all out of the cabin and came up, I found the

William Elder Buist

William Elder Buist came to America from Scotland in 1883 as an 18-month-old child. Babies and young children were especially at risk for disease and malnutrition. Most of the people who died aboard ships crossing the ocean were either young children or elderly adults.

vessel all broken up into fragments except the cabin. Water was rushing at a furious rate [into the cabin], sweeping out all the partitions. A great many of us was still clinging to the poop [deck]. After a while I made my escape to the rocks upon the broken fragments of the vessel. . . .

We passed a dreadful night sitting on some of the broken masts, up to our [waists] in water. At daylight we were all very busily engaged [in] picking up such provisions [from the damaged ship] as could be found.

A very small island or two was seen about 6 miles distant. Having one [small row]boat, with a little repairing, some were soon able to go and view the land. The islands was small, three in number, without inhabitants, barren and desolate. A few coconuts were the only things growing that was fit to eat. With these & some turtles and birds, [and] with the little we picked up from the wreck, we managed to live.

On the 20th November, our [row]boat being repaired, the captain and crew started for Tahiti. And on the 2nd of December, to our great joy, [they returned with] a vessel for our deliverance. We embarked on the 3rd and got to the island of [Huahine] on the [11]th where we saw the grave of Sister [Esther] Allen who [had died from childbirth during a previous successful voyage of the *Julia Ann* and] was buried on that island. We stopped there three days. We then went on to Tahiti where we landed on the 19th. When we got there the [government] consuls would do nothing for us.

The American Consul said he had nothing to

do with us because we were English subjects. The English Consul said he had nothing to do with us because we were in an American ship. So we were in a very peculiar situation with [our] friends, without [a] home, without clothes, without food, and in a strange land under the French government.

By the charity of the Free Masons Lodge we were [given] food until the 19th of Jan., when they could feed us no longer. We then went to the English Consul again and he has [given] us food ever since. But he says he shall [discontinue feeding us] at the end of this month's stay. When we shall get away from this place, I know not.

We ha[ve] three orphan children stopping with us, Eliza and Francis Humphries and Maria Harris who wish to be remembered to their friends, if you should have the chance to see any of them.

There is but very little work for a man to get in this place. Mother and Father and we all are in good health though we have lost all our worldly goods. Yet, we have faith in God and trust he will deliver us soon from this wicked place. I hope to see you all before long in the land of [the] free surrounded by the Saints of the Most High God. Mother, father, and Stephen join me in sending our love to you all, likewise remember us to all friends.

Please let Brother [Augustus] Farnham know of the wreck, also of our situation. Do not grieve yourself.

I remain your affectionate,

Peter Penfold

Peter and his family arrived safely in California. Nothing is known of his later life.

SOURCE: Letter of Peter Penfold in Diary of Augustus Farnham, 56–57. LDS Church Archives. See also, Penfold, Peter. Letter. In the Zion's Watchman *(the Australian Mission periodical), May 24, 1856, 77–78.*

PART FIVE

A New Home

*"I have had a great desire to go on and progress in the Church and
Kingdom of God in the forthcoming year and gather up to Zion for
which I have set out for. I have $24 towards it."*
—John James Fry

When the long-awaited words "Land Ahoy!" were heard
Latter-day immigrants knew that they had completed only
the first part of their long journey. Those headed to Utah
from East Coast ports still had more than two thousand miles
to travel by train, river steamer, wagon, handcart, or foot.

As they disembarked from the ship to be examined by health

officials and given clearance to be on their way, young pioneers experienced a variety of emotions. Those traveling with their families could hold on to a sister's hand or mother's skirt and feel a sense of security, even in a very new world. But a significant number of children and teenagers traveled apart from their families. Their parents and siblings were already in Utah or were still back in the "homeland." To these young people, America must have seemed both exciting and very confusing. Surely, during their separation from family, these lonely little travelers would imagine the "grand reunion" they would one day enjoy with their loved ones.

In the Territory of Utah, these remarkable young pioneers would witness a desert "blossoming like a rose." With their bare hands they would help build temples, stores, schools, and theaters. They would build homes for their families, grow crops, tend livestock, and make clothing, butter, candles, and farm tools.

Many of these young ocean-crossing immigrants would again board a ship years later, this time to return to their native lands as missionaries, to preach the gospel that had so dramatically changed their own lives. "Zion" had once meant a destination in the tops of the mountains, but "Zion" would also come to mean a condition of the heart, a commitment, and a spiritual goal.

In the century ahead and beyond, Zion was to be established in villages, cities, and countries all over the world, preparatory to the second coming of the Savior. And these young travelers helped lay the foundation for that work in a most wonderful and remarkable way.

Wedding picture of Emily Chadwick and Frederick Zaugg

Frederick Zaugg

"To make the Lord my friend."

BORN: April 26, 1869, Vaud, Switzerland
PARENTS: Frederick and Elizabeth Lobsiger Zaugg
SAILING DATE: May 17, 1884
SHIP: *Arizona*
AGE: 15

Elder Gottlieb Hirschi from Dixie, Utah, came [to our house in Erlach, Switzerland,] one evening looking troubled in mind and spirit. My mother showed sympathy and interest in what might be the cause of his sadness and was told that a letter from his brother, Christian Hirschi, of Park Valley, Box Elder County, Utah, had brought the sad news to him saying that his brother had lost five out of his six children with diphtheria in a little over one week. Two died in one day, the oldest son was unharmed.

This news brought sadness and wonderings to the family. The two Hirschis were born in Switzerland, accepted the gospel, and immigrated to Utah. Now

It was early in the morning of the 16th of July [1864] when the words "Land Ahoy!" were heard and it was a lively rush on deck to witness the new land, and it was certainly a picture never to be forgotten. After our six weeks and over of an ocean life, to again witness land, it looked to us beautiful. In a few short hours a pilot had us in a tow and we were safely taken into the harbor of New York. Here we were interviewed by the customs officers and were placed in the Castle Garden, where all were examined as to health and inquiries made to comply with the U.S. laws as to our right to land. After passing a critical examination, we were passed and permitted to go ashore.

—*Charles William Symons emigrated at age 18, in 1864, aboard the* Hudson.

the question came as to why the Lord would treat good Saints so severe. Elder Hirschi said, "It is no doubt the will of the Lord."

About six weeks later Elder Hirschi returned to our family. He had another letter from his brother inquiring if there might be a boy of good Mormon parents who would like to come to Zion and live with his family; if so he would pay his fare or transportation if he were not over 12 years old, so he could come for half fare. I thought why could I not be that boy. I am 15 but no bigger than a 12 year old. Elder Hirschi promised he would see the mission office.

I waited and I prayed that it might be me. I had a feeling I was that boy. I prayed to the Lord that his will be done. In the month of April, 1884, word came from the mission office in Bern, Switzerland, for father and mother to bring their son to the office. Bern was more than 30 miles from Erlach. This meant a big day's journey.

Father was very busy and could not very well spare two days so mother and I made the trip. We went by way of Grissenberg where there lived an uncle, (mother's brother) who inherited the old home. We remained overnight and left early the next day. We arrived at the office near noon and met the president who received us kindly and assured mother that I could go to Zion. The company would leave on the 14 of May 1884. We could sign all papers on that day.

We remained with a family of Saints overnight and next day we went as far as Grissenberg, [to] my uncle's, and remained overnight. Mother received no encouragement from her brother to let me go to America, especially to the Mormons.

He told her she would not see me again. "Well I am sure I will see him again if not in this world then across the curtain for I am sure now that Jesus is the Christ and that he is alive and is the Father of our Salvation and will eventually bring us to God. I am trusting him with all I have, even my son." To this [he] smilingly remarked, "We will see. Time will tell." We left and were soon on the way. We got home alright and the news went the rounds, but in [our] home, tears of sorrow and of joy were freely shed.

The month was spent in preparation for the great journey to Utah, and I spent some time working with father and mother helping them hoeing weeds. Father and mother both encouraged me to hope for the best that we may meet again in the due time of the Lord and in a more friendly world. I bid farewell to my school mates. It was hard, but we were prepared for it by the spirit of truth which we now enjoyed.

I bid farewell to my school mates, some of them were nice about it, sincere, and others sneered and had some funny remark to make; all wondered what would happen to me. One of my teachers gave me a good handshake and said, "Fred, I don't see that you could better yourself with the Mormons. They live in a city on the shores of a great salt sea. They have a wall 40 feet high around it and name their city Salt Lake City. They will keep you a slave." I answered, if the people are as good as the Mormon missionaries, I would not care if I never got out.

The day of parting had come. After bidding my brothers and sisters farewell, again we walked the 30 miles to the capital. Mother had prepared my luggage which consisted of a pair of pants,

Landing at Castle Garden [New York] was a real adventure, [all] the hustle and the bustle, crowds meeting crowds, boxes to be opened and examined, people disappointed because friends were not there and so on. My father was there, however. It was almost dark and I was looking up through a jam when I heard, "There she is with her dear little face." I think our family must have made a good impression with the ship's officers, for when it came our turn to have the luggage examined, the word was passed on that we were alright.
—*Ruth May Fox emigrated at age 13, in 1867, aboard the Louisiana.*

After a long and tiresome voyage, we arrived in New York Harbor on the morning of July 4th. [Since] that was a holiday we had to remain on board until the next day. We had a splendid view of the fireworks that night from the ship as we lay in the harbor.

—Henry Crane emigrated at age 13, in 1866, aboard the American Congress.

two shirts, a blanket, and a few trinkets of personal interest; all put in a carpet bag with a few cakes, a sausage, some chocolate, and a flask [of brandy] to prevent being seasick. These trinkets were bought in Bern. The most precious gift of all was the good and loving counsel of my dear mother which came before me when trouble and disappointment came. [She counseled me] to make the Lord my friend, which could only be done if I was also his friend. Confide in the Redeemer and pray always. Be honest in all dealings, be pure and clean.

My father and a friend came [to say goodbye] a few minutes before the train pulled out. They were on the road nearly all night and seemed quite tired. I began to fear they would not get here, but thankful that I could see [my father] and take his hand. The train pulled out. We waved white handkerchiefs until a mountain shut out our vision.

Now I realized what I was doing and what my work and my promises to my family was, and [that] I must not fail. For a moment I wept, and friends tried to comfort me. I began to face the prospects of whatever was in store and made the best of things as I came to them. I was now with a company of Latter-day Saints all bound for Zion, which made travel congenial. We remained in the city of Basel overnight [and] picked up more Saints from that locality. I slept on the floor with my knapsack for a pillow and the blanket over and under me.

[The] next morning we left Switzerland and were on our way to the city [of] Antwerp in Holland [now in Belgium], where we arrived in the evening. The ship was there and we all got on

Over 1,250 Saints crossed the Atlantic on nine voyages aboard the steamship Arizona.

and had the first meal on the ship. [During] the night the ship went across the North Sea and was in a terrible storm. I felt that I might be sick, so I went on deck and I sat on a hatch that was sheltered and it was warm; no one seemed to notice me so I prepared for what may come. The waves were getting bigger and bigger until the prow [front] of the ship would bury itself in the water of the oncoming wave. Then the ship raised again and a wave of water five or six foot high rolled along over the deck toward me, but it spilled off the deck before it reached me. It was thrilling and awful.

We were all safe and no one was hurt, but all but me were seasick. I was fresh and happy and saw a wonderful sight. I never saw water that wild, nor could I believe it could be so rough. This was only the North Sea. What would it be on the Atlantic Ocean? The ship landed at Hull, the passengers proceeded to Liverpool by train.

We arrived at the great seaport. My eyes saw ships as [many as] the stars in the heavens, all sizes large and small. When all lit up at night it

We landed at Castle Garden, New York, June 2, 1865, and found the country in deep mourning over the tragic death of Abraham Lincoln. Everywhere we saw soldiers who were returning home from the Civil War. I remember one troop carrying what remained of a huge American flag. The center had been taken out by a cannon ball, and soldiers were carrying it down the street by its corners. They looked ragged, tired and sick as they dragged themselves down the street to their quarters amid the sound of cheers and martial music.

—Mary Ann Greenhalgh Mace emigrated at age 17, in 1865, aboard the Belle Wood.

looked like the milky way in the heavens. We saw our ship which would take us to the great land of Zion, the *Arizona,* a ship provided with steam power and sails.

Great stacks of crated oranges [were] in the warehouses. I could not get any but I smelled them. I wondered what they would taste like, [but] I never tasted any. We were allowed on the ship as soon as we complied with all regulations. Our first meal was supper and I ate as a hungry boy, but it seemed to me everything tasted and smelled like fish. Of course most Latter-day Saints were riding steerage or third class. We had picked up some [passengers] in Holland and quite a number of English and Danes. Most of us were quartered two stairs down where our windows were submerged. We all were in a big room with sleeping accommodations like a dormitory, or bunks with poor mattresses. We furnished our own bedding.

We all knelt in prayer before retiring. One led in prayer. We asked the Lord to protect the great ship with all its people that all [might] arrive in the great land of America and continue with us to Utah till we meet our friends and dear ones. And to bless President [John] Taylor, the Prophet of the Lord. We then retired for the night.

The great ship left Liverpool during the night and we were awakened in the morning to get our breakfast. This was brought to the steerage passengers in baskets, kettles and [on] trays. We had to have our own tins, knife, fork and spoon, and a cup. We had no table, chair or other accommodation. The food was dished out to each and was plenty, oatmeal with syrup, biscuit and butter, a piece of bacon and all the sea biscuits we wanted. We were not allowed on deck, but had a place to get fresh air on the prow of the ship where we could see over the water. We had favorable winds towards the promised land, the Zion of our ideals. Everyone was in good spirits and made ourselves at home. Meals came regular. [For] dinner we had soup, vegetables and meat, pudding for dessert, and hot rolls.

The ocean was now getting rough and the ship became like a toy tossed about and the waves played with it. Our belongings rolled about the floor and soon we had to put everything on the bunk and tie it down or sit down on it. The water began to come down the vent pipes and was getting over all the floor. We had to raise our feet to keep them dry. And so it went, into the night, and there was weeping and [excitement] and fear. I commenced to sing "How Firm a Foundation, Ye Saints of the Lord," [and] all joined in singing. We sang several [other] hymns. Fear left, the pumps [kept] the water from rising any higher, the winds seemed to ease up some, but it was difficult for the stewards to bring our eats and more difficult for some of the Saints to hold the food on their plates. It was no joke.

The [weather] changed [and] the sailors began their chanting. I wondered what was happening. I worked my way to the main deck and saw the sailors pull on the ropes to set the spars,* so the sails would fill with wind. Just at [that] moment, someone grabbed me by the neck and the seat of my pants and held me over a railing. I looked at the dark green waters [and] a thrill went through me. I was glad my pants did hold to bring me on deck again and set me on my feet. I did not know what language he spoke, but I understood it and

The hustle and bustle of a port city

hastened down the stairs. Evidently I had changed color, for my people asked me, "What is the matter with you? You are pale." I had a good reason for it. I related my experience. I was glad I could.

In a little over eight days we had made the trip from Liverpool to New York. About 1 P.M. the ship anchored about a mile from shore. We passed the remaining night on deck. No one was seasick any more. We saw the Brooklyn Bridge

---

* *A stout pole to support one of the sails*

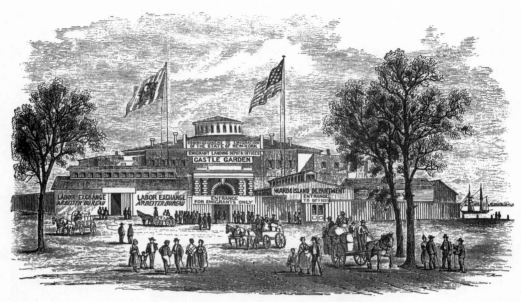

Castle Garden was the immigration depot for over 65,000 Saints who passed through its doors between 1840–1890.

After five weeks and four days one morning we sighted land. I don't think Columbus and his crew were any more pleased than we were. The ship docked at Castle Garden, and we were herded like sheep to street cars, and were put on the train. Talk about rough riding. I don't think a trip down Lake Creek Canyon on a wagon load of wood was any worse.

—*James Lindsay emigrated at age 10, in 1862, aboard the John J. Boyd.*

with its crown of gas lights. It had just been dedicated. It was a beautiful sight and a wonder. It was a wonderful thing to anticipate putting my feet on this wonderful and great land of America.

Morning came. The pilot ship brought the inspectors [and] doctors to inspect the passengers and cargo of the ship. The pilot ship led the way and we landed and went through Castle Garden to have our citizen's papers examined, and [to] declare our intentions, [and] also to what part of the country we each are going, etc. The passengers were unloaded in the order of class, first, second, and third.

We boarded a train that was standing by on a ferry. When all the passengers were on, the ferry pulled for shore. [The train] left the ferry and was now on a main [rail]line to Chicago. After a while we came to St. Louis [Missouri] and crossed over a bridge that spanned the mighty Mississippi [River]. The muddy water was almost up to the rails. The train went very slow through the great prairies. I had my eyes open for buffalo, but saw none. But we saw thousands of antelope and then the great Rocky Mountains.

And we now saw the Great Salt Lake and the Valley that inspired Brigham Young to say, "This is the place." [We] arrived in Ogden in the afternoon of the first of June 1884, where many friends were waiting for their emigrant friends. It was a great sight to see. Brother, sister, husband and wife, sons and daughter, met each other again after being separated for a time. Can I someday in the future experience such an unspeakable joy? Now for a moment I was home. Then, [I] looked around again for the friend I [had] never seen, but I looked in vain. No one seemed to have a claim on me. All had departed. I was left alone. I knew not what to do. It was now night, nearly eleven o'clock. I entered the little station with long benches against the wall, and thought I could pass the night there.

[Then] I heard someone calling Box Elder. It was a conductor announcing stations along the Utah Northern Railroad. I got on the train, unobserved, and sat down. The train was now on the way and the conductor examined the passenger tickets. He came to me [and] I shook my head. He asked for money, I handed him my purse. He looked in it and saw only 25 cents. He handed it back to me and went on through the train, then came back and sat down beside me. "Where are you going?" "Me? Box Elder." [Frederick could not speak or understand much English.] Soon the train stopped at the station

Father was not long in finding the ship that we [were] to sail in and I was delighted at the idea of being on the water in such a big ship. It was all fun and pleasure for me, but I was in and out and everywhere where I had not ought to be and kept my parents in hot water all the time till we got ready to sail on the 13th day of May.

—*Heber Robert McBride emigrated at age 13, in 1856, aboard the* Horizon.

Box Elder. The conductor took my handbag and beckoned me follow. He went into the office and conversed with the officer who made known by the clock he would take me somewhere at 12 o'clock.

The train went on, and the agent took my pack behind the desk and took me along a broadway with trees on each side. [We went on] quite a long walk, then stopped in front of a small house on the left side of the road. [The agent] knocked on the door [and] a gentleman in his night clothes came to the door. The two conversed together and the agent went back to the station. The old gentleman shut the door and made a light and put his trousers on and came and asked me in. He tried to talk with me, but it was not understandable. He brought some bedding in and made a bed on the kitchen floor and bid me lay down. He brought me some bread and milk, but I could not eat. The man took it away and put the light out, and I was soon asleep. I awakened as soon as it was light and picked up the bedding and went out. I looked around wondering in which direction Park Valley might be. I wondered if it was beyond these great mountains.

After a hearty breakfast of bacon and eggs, fried potatoes, radishes and bread and butter, and a glass of milk, I took a leaf from my notebook and wrote on it in German and French, so someone could read and inform me where Park Valley is. I signed my name and indicated where I am from. This good man took the note and went into the city and found George Grael, the county clerk. This man had been on a mission in Switzerland, in the French speaking part, and could speak French. This man came back with the elder man, and when he saw me he said "Bonjour messier, coma ca va." Well, once more, I could understand. It was like an angel's voice. Soon we were in a conversation. He took me to his home where I was treated as one of the family.

After inquiring of people who knew of Park Valley, we found it to be about 75 miles west of Box Elder (now Brigham City). In order to get there, I would have to go back to Ogden and take the train . . . to Kelton. The ticket [would] cost $6 dollars and I would still have 25 miles on a wagon trail to get to Park Valley. I drew a long breath. George Grael then said "Just be patient and time will always bring things about. You are welcome to be with us until you can get in touch with your party." This made me happy again knowing that the Lord does not forsake anyone that does his will.

One day I noticed two roan horses drawing a covered wagon along Main Street. Two [men were] sitting in a seat, and one I knew. It was a young man that came in our company. His name is Christian Barfus. I ran to the wagon and the Mr. Barfus introduced me to Brother [Christian] Hirschi [the man I was seeking] and said "this is Fred Zaugg." This was a happy meeting. I ran back to the house, got my few things, and thanked these good people. Brother Greal was away. I bid them farewell and continued my quest for Zion. So far I had seen but little of the Zion of my imagination. We traveled along a dusty road. It was hot and dry and I was looking for a drink of water. On the other side of

The Colorado, *a side-wheel paddle steamboat, brought Latter-day Saint travelers up the Missouri River to Nebraska in 1865.*

Corinne by a little mountain was a little stream of water running across the road. I jumped off the wagon and dropped on my stomach, and took a swallow and almost passed out. It was terrible, salty and bitter. Surely this cannot be Zion.

I kept my thoughts in me and went on. We got on top of Promontory [summit and] stopped at a nasty spring where cattle had been drinking. Mr. Hirschi had water with him to . . . drink. This spring was named Cedar Spring. Mr. Hirschi prepared supper and Barfus and I tended to the horses and hobbled them. There was plenty of nice grass. After supper we made a bed of cedar boughs to place quilts on. It made a real soft bed. In the night I was awakened by the howling of wild animals. Brother Hirschi said they were wolves. Will they hurt us? No, he said, they may not come near. . . . Nothing happened and daylight came again. Mr. Hirschi got breakfast and Barfus and I brought back the horses.

After breakfast we were on the way again. Sagebrush and cedar, jackrabbits, rattlesnakes, and many kinds of wild animals were along our way. [We saw] great Salt Flats with nothing growing on them. Our trail was along the railroad and we finally came to Monument Point, west of Promontory where the Eastern and the Western Railroad companies met and joined as one great company just 15 years before. We spent the night at Locomotive Springs, several large streams of water from great lava cracks. The water was also salty and it was a breeding place [for] mosquitos. They were very bad. Who could live in a place like this?

We passed the night some way, and [were] ready for the last lap and over the last hill, when we got a glimpse of Zion, the promised land. On and up, away from the great lake bottom, over hills and dales. Now we reached the last hill. Mr. Hirschi said, "When we get on the top of this hill you will get a view of Park Valley." I drew a long breath—"Is this Zion?" I asked. "Yes, when you make it," he answered. These words left a deep impression in my mind. "If you make it," became my motto. Things we like to live in and enjoy, we have to make. If we want a friend, we must love him. If you want a favor of the Lord, you must serve him and keep his commandments and the blessings will come by going after them.

Frederick worked for Mr. Hirschi in Park Valley, Utah, for nearly three years to pay off his immigration debt and then to pay for his three sisters and two brothers to emigrate to Utah. He also worked at a hotel in Terrace, a nearby railroad town. Unfortunately, his parents died before they had a chance to join their children in Utah. Frederick married Emily Chadwick on March 5, 1891, and they became the parents of thirteen children. They farmed in Park Valley; Sterling, Alberta, Canada; LeGrande, Oregon; and West Point, Utah. Frederick served two missions for the Church in Germany, in 1900 and 1920. He was very musical; he played the accordion, mouth organ, and he loved to yodel. He died August 17, 1956, and is buried in Syracuse, Utah.

SOURCE: *Zaugg, Frederick. Autobiography. Typescript, 20–33. Original in private possession.*

Charlotte Ann Hillstead (Bates)

"This was the happiest time of my childhood."

BORN: December 31, 1858, Hull, Yorkshire, England
PARENTS: John Blakey and Charlotte Gray Hillstead
SAILING DATE: June 1871
SHIP: *Wyoming*
AGE: 12

I think this was the happiest time of my childhood. My parents were busy getting ready to go to Utah. They had money enough to bring their large family, ten of us, to America.

We were so excited. Mother had been told what kind of clothes to make for us to travel in. They sold the bakery and furniture, and at last we got started. We went by train to Liverpool where we were to take the ship. I could see it a long way from the shore. We left Liverpool near the last of June, 1871. They took us in a small boat to the ship. I think they called it the *Wyoming*. Here we were to stay for ten days.

We were steerage passengers. The missionaries were cabin passengers. One

I well can remember the first step that I made on American soil. I had been taught to believe that it was a land of promise, blessed above all other lands and although a small boy of fifteen years of age I felt like thanking God for the blessings I then enjoyed.

—*George Cunningham emigrated at age 15, in 1856, aboard the* Thornton.

of them would bring us a cake or a walnut. We thought that was fine.

My youngest sister and I were always together. I was fair with light hair and blue eyes. She had dark eyes and hair. We thought the food was very poor. I was seasick for a few days. It seemed strange to look around and see nothing but water. One morning we went on deck we could hardly see each other as the fog was so thick and they kept the fog horn going all the time. They were afraid of being hit or of hitting some other ship. It was several days like that. One morning we went on deck. The fog had passed away and the sea was like blue glass and we could see New York.

Before we could leave the ship we had to line up and be vaccinated. Someone had the smallpox on the ship. We landed on what they called Castle Garden, but I did not see a castle nor a garden. It was just a big wooden shed with a roof across it and we stayed there two or three days. Mother was afraid to let us go away. We might get lost.

We landed on the 4th of July. It was the first time I saw firecrackers. The thing that appealed to me was the way the little girls dressed. They wore high top shoes. They looked wonderful to me. There were fruit stands there on which were the first peaches, apricots, and tomatoes I had ever seen. My brother saw the tomatoes and bought some. He took one bite and spit it out and gave me the rest. I thought it was like poison. It was many years before I learned to like tomatoes. We stayed for several days sleeping on the floor in Castle Garden. I suppose those who had money went to hotels but we had plenty of company, all nationalities. But we didn't care. We were going to Zion to be with the people of God and mingle with the prophets of God and his people.

We left New York and started for the West. We were not like the emigrants who had to walk all the way. I think we were about ten days on the train. We arrived in Salt Lake City about the 20th of July. It was in the evening after dark. I remember passing on South Temple and looking down Main Street. They had boardwalks and a small ditch on each side of the street with water running down it. They had lamp posts with lamps lit up all the way down the street. One of the missionaries, Milford Bard Shipp, took us to his home for a day or two until we could get located some place. The next day some friends of father's and mother's named [Joseph F.] Smith [and his wife] came to see us and said they had a house we could live in as long as we wanted it. There was a log room and a lumber room, so we moved in.

The Hillstead family homesteaded 120 acres of land in Tooele Valley, Utah. Charlotte married Myron William Bates December 22, 1877, in the Endowment House in Salt Lake City. They became the parents of eight children. Charlotte was a widow for nearly fifty-three years and survived all of her children but one. She loved serving in the Relief Society and did a considerable amount of temple work for her ancestors. She died April 11, 1952, and is buried in Salt Lake City.

SOURCE: "The Life of Charlotte Ann Bates," 2–3. LDS Church Archives. Also, Charlotte's obituary in the Deseret News, *12 April 1952, in possession of Barbara W. Whiting, Provo, Utah*

Alfreda Marina Oceana Larson

Alfreda Marina Oceana Larson was born September 8, 1874, as her family sailed across the Atlantic Ocean. Her father, Ola Larson, named her Alfreda. The doctor on the vessel named her Marina, which means "born on the water." And the captain gave her the name of Oceana.

Brigham Henry Roberts

"Polly, this ship won't sink."

BORN: March 13, 1857, Warrington, Lancashire, England
PARENTS: Benjamin and Ann Reed Everington Roberts
SAILING DATE: April 30, 1866
SHIP: *John Bright*
AGE: 9

"Harry," as he was called by his family, and his sister Mary, age sixteen, crossed the ocean with a group of other Mormon emigrants. Their father remained in England; their mother had gone to the Salt Lake Valley four years earlier and was anxiously awaiting their arrival.

It was a varied crowd of passengers milling on the main open deck before the sailing of the ship, and there were both tears and laughter in the matter of saying goodbye, as many of those who came aboard were relatives of the passengers. I noticed that my sister Mary was for most of the time in tears, and it was a matter of wonderment with me why she should be crying. For me the secret thought was that I was now on the way of fulfilling the promise I had given my mother, that I would join her in America, "Zion" to the [Latter-day] Saints. That thought filled me with

very great satisfaction. Although nothing was said between us on that head, I could only account for my sister's tears by supposing that she was afraid that the ship might go down. While clinging to her hand as she went among her friends bidding them goodbye, I stamped firmly on the strong open deck, and finally getting her attention, I said, "Polly (for that was the family name for Mary) Polly, this ship won't sink." She gave tearful assent. Some time late in the afternoon, the vessel was cleared of visitors, the anchor "weighed" and the ship started upon her voyage. . . .

Many of the May [voyage days were] cloudless and the air balmy. There were frolics on the deck, games and group singing, and there were many beautiful voices in that list of passengers, English, Welsh, Scottish—for they had been gathered from all the scattered branches in those countries, some of them noted for their music. There was dancing, also games for the children; among others, marbles for the boys when the ship was steady enough for the marbles to stay in the rings until shot out by the players.

There was seasickness plenty. Some of the people being sick all the way, though I was in my element all the time and the harder the wind did blow the better I enjoyed myself. When the big waves made the ship toss about, I was not seasick any of the time. When land was sighted, I almost felt sorry.

—*Heber Robert McBride emigrated at age 13, in 1856, aboard the* Horizon.

We arrived in the States in the year 1849, and as we were going up the river to Iowa, my little sister died, and we were forced to land that we might bury her. I was about five years old, and the burial service made a deep impression upon me. We first settled in a neighborhood where there were no little children, and the Scottish settlers thought I was a "fine wee lassie," so [they] asked mother to let me visit them for a day, which she did, but I returned with the germs of the "itch." Soon the whole family had contracted the disease. Mother was much troubled and worried, for this was a new disease for her.

—*Ann Jane Willden Johnson emigrated at age 4, in 1849, aboard the* Zetland.

Of course there were childish quarrels and violence too. I remember one which arose over the dispute about giving up of marbles that had been lost to me in the play, for the game was generally for keeps. The boy with whom the quarrel arose was of dark complexion, swarthy skin. A hard face it would have been called because of its desperate earnestness and the fury with which he held up the fight of his quarrel. First blows were struck; but "Blackeye" [a sailor who seems to have been assigned to watch over the children on the ship] was back at hand and soon separated us. The dark complexioned boy's name was John Gibbs, and he and I were held apart by "Blackeye." There was great anger registered on each face. Strange was the meeting of us two under such circumstances. Twenty years shall not have passed when John Gibbs will have become a martyr to the faith of the Latter-day Saints, and I, presiding over a mission in the Southern States, will take some risks in bringing John's body from an unsatisfactory burial to send it home from Tennessee to friends in his hometown in Utah. The identification of each other and the relation of the circumstance [of the marble game and quarrel] to our lives, took place during our missionary experience together. It can't often be prophesied what future relations quarreling boys will have to each other. This was one of the strangest.

So far as [I can remember], the officers of the *John Bright* were very fine, and they watched with serious care over the welfare of their passengers. This is true of all of them. Perhaps one exception was the first mate, who was a "grouch" both towards the crew and the passengers. Maybe he was a splendid officer too, but he shouted out his words in a deep guttural or husky voice, and always had the appearance of having got up feeling mad about something. One mid-afternoon, he gave a gruff order to "Blackeye" to go and bring him some bread and butter and a cup of tea. He was on duty and wanted this refreshment. Presently, "Blackeye" came back with some choice, thinly-sliced white bread and butter laid together like sandwiches. The mate appeared angry that the slices of bread had been cut so very thin. Without any apparent reason, he shouted at "Blackeye" as he threw the bread and butter over the side of the ship into the ocean, "I told you to get some bread and butter, not wafers!" And when I recall the sea fare of the passengers, which did not include delicately cut bread and butter, it was with no slight indignation that I witnessed this action of the first mate. "Blackeye," however, went to the cook's quarters and soon returned with bread thick enough to please the first mate's taste. But if ever the ocean was begrudged a thin bread and butter sandwich, it was when it received that double sandwich from the hands of the angry first mate of the *John Bright.*

Harry and his sister arrived safely on the upper bay of New York on June 6, 1866. He now describes the scene and his physical appearance:

A lad midway between nine and ten years of age, I could be seen seated on a bench on the south side of Castle Garden. . . . I was a boy of no prepossessing appearance. In the first place I was clad in just a pair of barn-door trousers and jacket (made from the old trousers of an English

After eleven long weeks on the ocean we arrived in New Orleans and went on board a river steamer. We were many days going up the Mississippi River. A new dress that my mother had made me was blown over board into the river and was lost. I was broken-hearted over loss of it.

—*Elizabeth Grace McCune emigrated at age 7, in 1851, aboard the* Ellen.

It was with some peculiar feelings I first cast my eyes on this great American continent which land is a blessed land above all other lands on the face of the earth. The Lord has decreed and promised it to his people who will serve him and keep his commandments and if they will do right it will finally be given to them as an everlasting possession. May I be one among the number to obtain these blessings.

—*John Frantzen emigrated at age 19, in 1857, aboard the* Westmoreland.

policeman), a pair of iron-rimmed wooden clogs, and on my head was what was supposed to be a jaunty Scotch cap, faced with bright plaid around the rim and ending in two black streamers behind—a headgear which I heartily despised. My eyes were restless, keen, blue and deep set, my nose decidedly ill-shaped and upturned, and my face was freckled, my lips full, but not tender nor sweet. My head appeared to be crunched down into my shoulders, amounting almost to a deformity. My teeth were ugly, misshapen, with a wide gap between the two frontal ones through which I had learned to send forth a shrill whistle on occasion. My body was rather heavy, such as is described for lads as "chunky." My hair was of light mouse-colored hue, ill kept, slightly wavy and unruly of management—no amount of training seemed to affect it. On the whole I was stolid, and sober-faced. There was no joy in boyhood in

Interior view of Castle Garden

my appearance, no disposition to mill around with the seven hundred other emigrants thronging the Old Castle Garden. I seemed to be without companions and [they] doubtless would have been repulsed by me if they manifested friendliness. I was a boy evidently who was accustomed to being alone—apart from the throng. I was not restless, but rather solemn and gloomy.

By my side were several packages, some in canvas wrappings or small canvas bags. These proved to be pieces of fat-side bacon, made greenish by the intense pickling of the pork to make it suitable for food on the long voyage by the sailing vessel which had just ended. I also had some loaves of bread, some packages of hard tack. It had been a terrific voyage we had made on the ship *John Bright* of the Guion Line. The ship still lay some distance out in upper New York harbor.

From there, Harry and his sister traveled by river boat, train, and covered wagon to the Salt Lake Valley, where they arrived September 14, 1866. He describes the reunion he and his sister Mary had with their mother:

In the morning everybody [in our company] seemed to be up with the first streaks of the light of day over the eastern mountains, and in great haste in preparation to take up the journey. Breakfast seemed to be neglected, and there was not much to eat anyway. Before the sun rose, the [wagon]train, falling into its old line, swung down the low foothills until they struck a well-defined road leading into the city.

I was always ready to do all the errands. One day Father sent me to the kitchen. As I was running toward the cook-house, a wave struck the ship, it lurched and sent me spinning toward the rail. I grabbed some ropes just in time to save myself from going overboard. A sailor helped me up and said, "You sure missed going overboard that time." Everything on the stove was pitched off onto the floor. Everyone had to wait until the things were cleaned up and more dinner prepared before they could eat.

—*Agnes C. Hefferan Richardson emigrated at age 7, in 1865, aboard the* Belle Wood.

On our way crossing the ocean we witnessed many harrowing experiences. The sailors were really a tough lot, and would steal anything they could lay their hands on. In our group of Saints the men would take turns standing guard during the nights.

There were five people [who] died on the way over. We witnessed one man's body being thrown overboard. They wrapped him in a blanket and tied him on a slab, then tied a sack of coal to his feet then tossed it overboard into the ocean. It was a terrible sight. Some screamed, others fainted. It was the last time they let anyone witness this again.

—*Henry Peter Jacobs emigrated at age 12, in 1863, aboard the* John J. Boyd.

This entrance proved to be via Third South—then and long afterwards known as "Emigration Street," now Broadway. When Captain Chipman's ox team swung around the corner of Third South into Main Street, I found myself at the head of the lead yoke in that team, walking up the principal street of the city, the rest of the train following. Here the people had turned out to welcome the Plains-worn emigrants and were standing on the street sides to greet them. . . .

Along the road, perhaps nearly half way from the mouth of Parley's Canyon to the city, as I strode on ahead of Captain Chipman's team, I saw a bright-colored, dainty, charming little girl approaching me in the middle of the street. It was a strange meeting, we two. My hair had grown out somewhat. But three months' journey over the Plains and through the mountains without hat or coat or shoes for most of the way had wrought havoc with my appearance. My hair stuck out in all directions; the freckles seemed deeper and more plentiful and the features less attractive than when the journey began. Shirt and trousers barely clung to my sturdy form, and my feet were black and cracked but now covered by the shoes I had taken from the feet of a dead man at a burnt station. These I was wearing in compliment to my entrance into "Zion." Also my face had been more carefully washed that morning.

But try as I would, the shock of hair was unmanageable, and so no wonder the dainty little lady was somewhat timid in approaching me.

She had on her arm a basket of luscious fruit, peaches, plums, and grapes. These she extended to me, the "ugly duckling" of a boy from the Plains, and asked me if I would have some peaches. The answer was to gather up several which I strung along in the crook of my arm, and as soon as I had obtained what I supposed a reasonable portion, I wondered how I could get this fruit so wonderful back to Mary and at the same time retain my place in the march up Main Street. Pondering this question, of course unknown to the young girl who had brought me such a treasure, I finally turned back as best I could to the wagon where Mary was concealed under the wagon cover because of her being a little ashamed of her appearance. Running and climbing up on the tongue of the wagon, I called to my sister, handed to her the fruit, and then scrambled back to the ground and ran for my place at the head of the train and marched on until the head of Main Street was reached.

This then was the old Tithing Office behind the high cobble walls with its half round bastions and through a crude gateway on the west side of the block leading into the stock corrals of President Young, where most of the wagons of the train were driven and placed under the many straw-covered sheds that then occupied the place where the Deseret Gymnasium now stands. The cattle were soon freed from the yoke and seemed delighted with the straw and hay brought them.

Across the way on Temple Square block, the foundations of the temple rose above the general level of the surrounding ground and seemed to be an object of interest to nearly all the emigrants, many of whom were permitted to go

My mother took very sick and as the food was scorched or poorly prepared at times, she could not eat it and regain her strength. My brother Peter, who was 18 years old at the time, got a job helping the ship's cook. He used to secretly carry extra food to her. In time she got well, and always declared Peter saved her life.

—*Larsine Olsen Ottesen emigrated at age 6, in 1866, aboard the* Kenilworth.

All articles of food were in a raw condition except hard tack or ship's biscuits, which were not very enticing, it being necessary to break them with a hammer, and frequently in breaking them you would see many jumpers or maggots roll out of the crevices in the biscuit. The ship's rations consisted of salt beef, salt pork, potatoes, rice, split peas, and a very small quantity of flour; . . . salt, pepper, sugar, and we each had to be supplied with a linen bag to hold each of these articles, and at the time specified we were to be at the commissary to receive them.

—*Charles William Symons emigrated at age 18, in 1864, aboard the* Hudson.

within the wall and view it. By and by there were numerous meetings in various groups of people, friends of the emigrants, parents and sweethearts, and perhaps in some instances wives of the teamsters that had returned. There seemed to be an air of cheerfulness in all this meeting of people on the arrival of this large emigrant train of Saints.

Mary and I seemed to be so little part of this excitement and joy, because nobody seemed to come for us. Mary remained concealed under the wagon cover and I, lonesome and heartsick, sat upon the tongue of Captain Chipman's wagon, my chin in my hands and elbows upon my knees, thinking "Zion" was not so much after all, if this was all of it. The spirit of sadness, if it was not forlorness, settled upon me.

Presently, however, approaching from the west gate, I saw a woman in a red and white plaid shawl slowly moving among the hillocks of fertilizer that had been raked from the sheds and the yard. She seemed to be daintily picking her way, and there was something in the movement of her head as she looked to the right and to the left that seemed familiar to me. The woman was moving in my direction, and the closer she came the stronger the conviction grew upon me that there was my mother. I would have known her from the dainty cleanliness of everything about her.

I stood until she came nearly parallel to where I sat; then sliding from the tongue of the wagon, I said: "Hey Mother," and she looked down upon my upturned face. Without moving she gazed upon me for some time and at last said, "Is this you, Harry? Where is Mary?" Of course Mary was in the wagon, and I led my mother to where she was hiding, and when mother and daughter met, there was a flood of tears on both sides. At last I joined them, making the trio of the united family. It seemed difficult for our mother to realize that we at last were her children after more than four years of separation, but once in a while, a smile would break through the tears and she seemed to be extremely happy. A neighbor of hers, Brother John K. Crosby, a New Englander, had driven her from Bountiful to the city to get us children, and it took but a

short time to leave the remaining emigrant teams and people to find this wagon and make the start for home, Bountiful. . . .

There was one thing remembered in this reunion, and that was on my part. I felt that I had arrived, that I belonged to somebody, that somebody had an interest in me, and these were the thoughts that were in my mind as I sat in the wagon on the drive home to Bountiful.

As the wagon drew near to Bountiful, its clear-cut New England meeting house with a tower upon it seemed to loom large among the homes surrounding it, and before getting to it, I wondered if that was my mother's home. When the wagon passed it going eastward, without anything being said about its being her home, of course, I was sad with disappointment. I experienced a sense of great humiliation. Two blocks beyond it on the east, we came to the site of a log house with a dirt roof on one part of it and another part adjoining on the south that had been built up to the square with logs unchinked without a roof, and this, my mother turned to explain to me, was her home. But soon mother and children climbed out of the wagon and went into the house, and Brother Crosby drove away.

There were certain preparations made in the unroofed, annexed part of the log home, for presently my mother with a pleasant smile and a twinkle in her blue eyes took my hand and said, "Come with me my son; I haven't washed you for more than four years." After she got me into the open addition to the one-room cabin with hand bowl and towels, she stripped off [the] one shirt that had done duty for so long a time and started in to give me a scrubbing, which led me to believe that she was under the impression that I had not been washed since the last time she had washed me four years before.

What was left of the day was the wonderful meal prepared by [our other sister] Annie. Not much variety of food, for our mother was desperately poor, but what there was, was fit for princes—just white light buttermilk biscuits with butter, clear water from the creek, and dark, sweet, sticky fluid called "molasses." It was heartily enjoyed, Mary and me furnishing the principal appetites. How long the talk of the reunion lasted is not remembered, but it must have been far into the night. With the awakening of the next day, my life in Utah had begun.

Harry later became known as B. H. Roberts, who became President of the First Council of the Seventy at the age of thirty-one. A prolific writer of theology and history, he was elected to the United States Congress. He married Sarah Louise Smith, Celia Louisa Dibble, and Margaret Curtis, and was the father of fifteen children. He died September 27, 1933, in Salt Lake City.

SOURCE: *Roberts, B. H.* The Autobiography of B. H. Roberts, *edited by Gary James Bergera. Salt Lake City: Signature, 1990. Note: B. H. Roberts used third person pronouns (he, him, his) in his account when referring to himself. Bergera has changed them to first person (I, me, my). See also,* Autobiography of B. H. Roberts.

PART SIX

The Meaning of the Gathering

"I believed in the principal of the gathering and felt it my duty to go although it was a severe trial to me in my feelings to leave my native land . . . but my heart was fixed. I knew in whom I had trusted, and with the fire of Israel's God burning in my bosom, I forsook my home."
—Jane Charters Robinson Hindley

While reading the histories of young Latter-day Saints who left their homelands and crossed the oceans, we should remember the reason why they and their families were willing to undertake such a risky adventure. While peering over the railing of a sailing ship or steamer, many a young girl or boy must have dreamed of seeing a temple or a prophet. They also must have dreamed of life without religious persecution. Along with their parents and siblings, these young Latter-day Saints dreamed of a place to gather in safety to build the Lord's kingdom and help prepare the world for the second coming of Christ. They dreamed of Zion.

As Latter-day Saint children and teenagers became young adults, their spiritual feelings matured and they gained an even deeper appreciation for the gospel for which they had given so much. Those who helped bring them to their new home in the desert of the American West—parents, siblings, and friends, some of who gave their lives for their testimonies—clearly did not offer their sacrifice in vain. Through these children Zion would go forward, established and strengthened by a new generation of firm believers.

The history of Alma Ash reflects this transition to spiritual maturity and personal responsibility for the kingdom.

Alma Ash

"My prayer was that I could be faithful to God and His people."

BORN: February 10, 1861, Birmingham, England
PARENTS: Thomas and Sarah Ann Hick Ash
SAILING DATE: August 1, 1885
SHIP: *Wyoming*
AGE: 24

Whenever I saw [another Mormon] family emigrate to Zion, it used to cause very peculiar feelings to enter my heart. And oh, with what joy I [ponder]ed upon the gathering. The possibility of [our family emigrating to Zion in] the near future would give me the greatest joy. Indeed, I know of nothing which brought so much joy to my young heart as to talk about going to the [Salt Lake] Valley. Many times we young Mormon exiles (children of Mormon neighbors) played "Going to the Valley" by constructing a train and a ship and the like, of chairs and tables. [Then we would] imagine we were traveling along. I remember also keeping marbles and tops which I intended [to give] as presents to my companions who had already

The Mersey River at Birkenhead, England

We had no water except what was carried on the ship, and they used to haul it up, out of the bottom of the ship every morning, and we could have only so much a day. I was seven years old at this time—the oldest child in the family and I used to take the little tin pail and get our allotment for the day. We never sat down to a table while on board the ship.
   —*Maren Jensen Cutler Norton emigrated at age 7, in 1853, aboard the* Forest Monarch.

gone to the valley, and whom I expected to soon follow. I also kept tools which I thought would assist in the building of a house when we got to Utah.

Alma's father went alone to Utah in 1880, but returned to his family in England just five months later, after learning that his wife was expecting their eleventh child. Finally, with his family still facing financial difficulties, Alma and a companion decided to sail to America without their parents' knowledge.

We kept our plot [to immigrate to America] from our parents and did not tell a soul except [one] young man, Henry Phillips' brother William, and even he was kept off the scent as far as necessary, so that he did not know our real intentions.

It was the 31st of July when we left Birmingham on the London and Northwestern Railway for Liverpool. I well remember that it was in the evening about five or six o'clock when we gazed out of the window and looked over the place of our birth and boyhood. The town was as lively as ever [with] the noise and surging hosts of people. Each one went [about] his particular business or pleasure and little heeded the two half-frightened, sorrowful young men who had before them such a mission, and who were full of thought and bent on such a journey.

The thoughts that crowded our minds [were] fear and hope, faith and doubt. . . . It was now a fact—the long, long talk of [this] journey which we had planned but had never had the courage to carry out. Now we were fleeing with lightning speed across the lovely green country of our native land through hamlet and town, valley and hill until we reached the noisy, smoky city of ships, Liverpool.

I had [told my parents] we were going fishing for a couple of days at a friend's place who was a relative of Harry's—as my companion was familiarly called. It was the last holiday of the season in England and therefore we were going to make the best of it. But [for me] to go on a fishing trip, to my folks, was something peculiar, as I had never been known to indulge in such pleasures before. They, however, concluded it was alright.

I remember that just a few minutes before I left the house, I went upstairs to [see] my mother, for she was so sick that she had gone to bed. I wished her goodbye and said, "Take care and keep out of difficulty." Little did she realize that I

Thomas Henry White

Thomas Henry White emigrated from England in 1863, at the age of 16. He thought the food and water aboard the *Antarctic* was very poor. Before sailing, his mother toasted some of her homemade bread until it was very dry and put it in a sack. "We enjoyed this bread while it lasted," he wrote.

One thing amazed me very much in the new land—whenever I was introduced to as "just coming over" the salutation would invariably be "Oh, she's such a little greenhorn, is she?" That hurt my feelings for in England when I did the wrong thing they called me a little greenhorn.

—*Ruth May Fox emigrated at age 13, in 1867, aboard the Louisiana.*

should never come back to the humble little home sitting on Charles Henry Street. It was like pulling [my] very heart out to drag myself away for already there was a demand for money at home to tide us over. And never shall I forget the struggle I had to save the little means I had saved for this great event. Time and time again I was approached by my father and mother or sisters for money to help them. Time and time again I refused them or denied that I had any. This was something new to them as I had always given up my last schilling in a time of need which was nearly all the time. I clung to this little savings as if my life depended upon [it]. It was with an aching heart that I tore myself away from home and often times was I tempted to abandon the effort. I will here say that having a companion and friend gave me great encouragement

When we arrived at Liverpool we first made our way to the office of the Guion Line Steamship Company. We informed them that we wanted to find the docks and go aboard that night if possible, and asked them to direct us to 42 Islington, the office of the [LDS] Church in Liverpool, and which the Guion Company were very familiar with. Just as soon as we mentioned 42 Islington they treated us very politely and directed us where to go. We were soon on the way, and after walking some distance found the memorable office so well known to thousands of Saints and elders.

On the way to the office we tried to prepare ourselves in the best way we could by questioning ourselves as to the answers we might give President [Daniel H.] Wells if he chided us for coming away as we had done. We, however, were

The Guion Line carried over 40,000 Saints across the Atlantic, about ninety-eight percent of all LDS steamship passengers.

received by that genial and broad-minded soul with all kindness. He gave us a hearty welcome, and bade his wife, Sister Wells, to prepare a supper for us. He talked with us and counseled us and we held nothing from him. After supper he blessed us and bid us God-speed. We now felt very thankful to God for the favors shown us especially when we discovered that our course was not disapproved by the prophet of God in England. This gave us more joy and satisfaction than any money could have given us, for it lifted from our souls a load of doubt and we felt more cheerful and buoyant.

Now, it seemed as if the heavens were conspiring to bless us with good

The dock at Plymouth, England, 1863

things. We left the office and journeyed to the docks and after some little trouble we found the old ship, *Wyoming,* that was to bear us on safely and surely to the land of Ephraim. I always remember what a dark night it was, for we could only discern in the thick darkness the images of ships stretching out for miles like a forest. After rummaging on the old ship we found the head steward and he showed us a bunk where we laid down on the bare boards and talked to each other concerning our exploit until sleep closed our eyes for the rest of the night.

We woke in the midst of a noise and din occasioned by the preparations made by carpenters and others for the voyage. The clanking of chains and the . . . coarse voices, together with the hammering and so forth, soon reminded us of the reality of the scheme we had planned and thus far carried out. . . . At noon that day we sailed slowly and cautiously out of the docks and down the River Mersey as many thousands of Latter-day Saints have done before. I shall never forget the sensations experienced as the good old ship moved and crept along. Thousands of men and boys, women and girls were leaving work, for it was Saturday noon and according to the English custom these hands were through for the week. I must admit that most of these people seemed jovial and in comfortable circumstances.

In a little while we sat down on the deck and each wrote a few words to the folks at home telling them to be of good cheer and all would be well and that we had been impelled to take this course for the ultimate good of all. The next [day] was Sunday and the morning found us at Queenstown, old Ireland. Here we mailed our letters home and prepared our hearts for the sickness, monotony, and other incidents which generally accompanied a sea voyage of those times.

Our food on the boat was coarse and the care and attention given steerage passengers was almost brutal, for it was only those with cast iron stomachs and digestive organs which could eat the food and drink provided. We lay on the bare boards nearly the whole of the voyage. At

I recall that one stormy morning I awoke unable to find my clothing and shoes. The pitching of the ship had tossed my apparel out of the bunks and down the aisles and I had to recover my belongings from a heap of clothing piled at one end of our quarters.
—*Bertha Marie Jensen Eccles emigrated at age 10, in 1867, aboard the* Manhattan.

Sarah Elizabeth Bullock (Bissegger)

Sarah Elizabeth Bullock (Bissegger) was born on the sailing ship *Cynosure* on July 10, 1863, nine days before it arrived in New York. Her brother died of measles and was buried at sea just 30 minutes before Sarah was born. Her mother was so heartbroken over the death of her son that she had hardly any milk to feed her new baby. Sarah weighed less when the family arrived in the Salt Lake Valley than she did when she was born.

Liverpool we bought one straw bed thinking we could take turns by sleeping on it alternately, but this did not work so we cut it open and tried to make two beds of it and ultimately had to do without a bed.

A kind and considerate friend on board gave us a dollar and another two schillings. The journey, though only about ten days, seemed ten months for we scarcely knew what to do with the time, and no one ever hailed the sight of land with more joy than we two young men did.

Arriving in New York, we went to Castle Garden and waited there until the coming of Brother [James H.] Hart, the Church agent in New York. Brother [George F.] Hunter, who had charge of our company, came with Brother Hart and shook hands with us and treated us kindly. Of course, we wondered what Brother Hart would do, for President Wells had instructed Brother Hunter to tell Brother Hart to be sure and send us along if he could, and Brother Hunter was as interested in us as a man could be.

The sight of New York and the hurry and bustle of that modern Babylon, together with the indifference to anybody's welfare except their own, had already took a good deal of nerve out of us and we ask[ed] ourselves the question, "What shall we do if left in Chicago?," for our ticket only took us that far. Instinctively we said "God help us" and then collapsed, sat motionless and awaited the verdict. We heard Brother Hunter tell Brother Hart the message of Brother Wells, but he quickly shook his head and said to us, "Boys, I should be pleased to do it if I could." He turned away and left us alone in our glory. I said to myself, "Ah, it's the same old ghost which has followed me and my father's house all our lives, namely disappointment." I bit my lips to keep back the gush of tears which were ready to come. But no, for once the specter "disappointment" was driven away by the kindly angel of "hope" which came to our rescue. Brother Hart stepped but a few paces and then as if he had received a revelation, he turned suddenly around and said, "Boys, I believe I will help you along. Come over to my office on Battle Square in two hours and we will make arrangements to send you along." These words I shall never forget and the impression made upon us at that time will endure to all eternity, for God was surely over us and had favored all we had done so far.

After this we strolled around New York but did not go far away. We went up Broadway as far as the City Hall and saw the decoration all over the city in memory of General Grant who had been buried, I think, the day before. We saw the post office and some of the buildings of the great [news]papers like "The World" and "The Herald." Arriving at [Brother's Hart's] office we soon signed a note for each of our fares from Chicago to Salt Lake City. Brother Hart was more generous than we ever expected him to be, for he insisted upon us taking a few dollars to provide food for nearly a week's travel on the way, which we also gave a note for. And thus far on the journey we saw clearly the hand of God in our behalf. How is it that one can ever doubt God? Surely all men have been the recipients of great and wonderful favors.

In the evening of that same day we crossed the river in a boat to New Jersey. The next few days were intensely interesting to us. Never shall

The only way of going to and from the galley was by means of a large ship ladder. You can imagine the difficulty of carrying this hot food from the galley which was on the deck, down the ladder to our berths which were in the steerage. Fortunate indeed was the individual who was possessed with a good stock of patience, for it was surely needed under these trying circumstances.

—*Mary Lois Walker Morris emigrated at age 14, in 1850, aboard the* Josiah Bradley.

Once I frightened all those on deck by holding on to the rope and ducking down over the edge of the ship to see if I could touch the water with my toes.

—Sarah Ann Horsley emigrated at age 7, in 1882, aboard the Nevada.

I forget the wonderful sights of this great and marvelous country as we journeyed along. The heat was intense but still we could see that people paid but little attention to it, but bustled, worked, and hurried along as if it were the mildest time of the year. . . . It seemed about this time that everything was coming our way for here we had money to spare.

I will pass over the usual incidents of travel merely to say that when we arrived at Chicago we were thankful to God that our lot was not cast there indefinitely, for it seemed like a whirlpool of trouble. . . . We took great interest in everything we saw and especially that which pertained to the history and travels of our people. I well remember how we regarded Omaha and Council Bluffs. We looked upon these places as almost sacred. Many times we would imagine we saw the old ox teams and the handcarts as they wended their way along the prairies or waded through the streams and rivers and then struggled up the rugged hills. Oh, what a journey, we would say. No wonder that many grew sick and weary and laid them down to die. Yes, in our mind's eye we saw them in all conditions: burying their dead by the wayside; in the corral at the shade of the evening; at prayer and at the dance; and we instinctively thanked God for the faith which these Saints had, to do this work.

Everything seemed pleasant enough to us until we approached the Rocky Mountains sometime before we arrived at Evanston, and then we saw a country which wore a different dress, and the sight made us homesick. This was the first tinge of homesickness which I had felt. It seemed so rugged and barren and the whole country

Several companies of Saints traveled on the Mississippi River aboard the steamboat Alex. Scott.

looked as if it had leprosy, being covered with white alkali and nothing visible but a few huts here and there. The train could not travel fast enough for us and we longed to gaze on verdure and smiling fields once more.

Early Sunday morning we arrived at Evanston, and at noon sometime at Ogden. Late in the afternoon we were on our way to Salt Lake City and how we rejoiced and talked and wondered, and yet withal there seemed in my heart a feeling of unrest with a little disappointment at the kind of country we had to live in. I had heard the elders from Utah talk about it and my father had often said to his children that they would never see such a tame and lovely country as old England. I did not understand this until I saw the chains of everlasting and interminable hills of the great West. I remember well how dreary and forsaken the country looked west of the Jordan River in the direction of the Great Lake. But still, the excitement of the journey and the unspeakable [joy] at being in Zion, and [being] delivered in such a marvelous manner from Babylon, crowded out from my mind the thoughts of the barrenness of the place.

Arriving in Salt Lake City about 7:30 o'clock and it being Sunday night everything seemed still and solemn. The little Union Pacific depot was lit by the usual arc lights and the pale moon shed a wondrous divine light upon the whole city. The city in 1885 was somewhat more old-fashioned than at the time

Josiah Rogerson

Josiah Rogerson sailed from England to America in 1856 at the age of 15, aboard the Horizon. He crossed the Plains with the Martin Handcart Company and suffered greatly in the early winter storms they encountered.

I write, which is sixteen years afterwards, and many of the quaint old landmarks of the early fifties remained undisturbed.

Never shall I forget how our hearts throbbed with emotion as we peered all around us to catch a glimpse of the place and people, as silently our little company trudged along South Temple Street towards the tithing yard where we expected to stay until morning. Oh, how reverently we regarded everything and everybody, and so sacred did everything appear to us that we wondered almost how people could be rude or light-minded in such a sanctified city. We gazed up at the temple which was at that time about up to the roof with the towers just commenced and silently in our hearts we resolved to begin a new life with new ambitions. We felt that we were quite an important addition to them both. We spoke in a quiet manner, I may say in a whisper, for fear of appearing boisterous or in any manner unbecoming.

At the tithing yard we were received kindly and invited to eat and while doing so somebody telephoned to the fire department to learn something of a friend and companion of ours who had emigrated six years before. He was a member of the volunteer organization and happened to be there at the department when the message was sent. He soon appeared and was delighted to see us. In a few minutes we had wished our [traveling] party goodbye, which we have never seen or heard from since, and was on our way to [our friend's] parent's home. He led us along a great wide street lined with trees on either side and a bubbling stream of water running down either side of the street. It seemed as if we were in

Oldest known photograph of the Utah Central Railroad which was built in 1870 and used to bring many immigrating Saints from the Ogden depot to Salt Lake City.

paradise. The night was a warm one and very dry, and yet with all one could catch a beautiful breeze from somewhere, which refreshed both soul and body. The people sat upon the doorstep or upon the porch and chatted away the pleasant hours of the night. Young men and maidens dressed in summer costume sauntered along or stood in groups somewhere and laughed and chatted. Little children scampered around, some of them in bare legs and feet. The air was alive with the whistle of crickets and other insects, while the toads and frogs lent their croak to the perpetual din. But there did seem a peace and a plenty everywhere. This wide street, we afterwards learned, was called Brigham Street, or more properly East South Temple.

Our friend conducted us along other streets until we came to the one his folks lived on, which he informed us, whatever that might mean, was on the bench. When we arrived at our friends home we found his mother and father and other members of the family reclining in rocking chairs and chatting about things in general. I well remember how astonished I was to see his family so comfortable and prosperous. It seemed to me that from the glimpse of [their] surroundings, we [could conclude] these people were very comfortably off as to the things of the world. We were received kindly and were soon answering questions about the folks in the Birmingham Branch. We talked for some time and some of the boys said they were going to bed, and their bed was outside in the lot. They invited us to sleep outside and [we] readily consented. Taking us some quilts and things we laid down on the ground and soon were gazing at the stars in heaven. This was the first time in my life that I had slept outside. Of course such a thing would hardly be possible in England except upon very rare occasions when a dry spell would occur in the summer time. I confess that I enjoy[ed] the novelty of sleeping outside in the open air the first night in Zion.

Before we slept, I looked around until I had located the constellation of the great bear and the polar star which I had so often found and located in England. I was much impressed and my prayer was that I would or might be faithful to God and his people.

By working in Salt Lake City at ZCMI, Alma was able to earn and borrow enough money to eventually bring his parents, four brothers, and five sisters, all at one time, to Utah. His father established a shoe shop on Seventh Avenue. He eventually served a mission back to Birmingham, England, where he served as president of the Hockley Branch.

On June 6, 1889, Alma married Ellen Sanford, who had also emigrated from England. They became the parents of seven children. Alma became an attorney in 1900, graduating highest in his class when he passed the state bar exam. He served a six-month mission to Tooele to organize the Young Men's Organization of the Church in that area. Alma died of typhoid pneumonia on January 10, 1902, in Salt Lake City, Utah. He was only thirty-nine years old. Alma is a great-uncle of Elder Neal A. Maxwell, a member of the Quorum of the Twelve Apostles of The Church of Jesus Christ of Latter-day Saints.

SOURCE: *Ash, Alma. Autobiography, 25–31. LDS Church Archives. Another excellent general source on the Ash family is* Ashes to Ashes, *compiled by Renae Sorensen Chase. Yorba Linda, CA: 1989.*

Epilogue

By the end of the nineteenth century, the leaders of The Church of Jesus Christ of Latter-day Saints began to encourage newly baptized converts overseas to create Zion in their native country, rather than immigrate to the Rocky Mountains of the American West. As a result, congregations of Latter-day Saints were established and began to multiply on every continent of the world.

As the era of large companies of Latter-day Saints sailing and walking to Zion ended, a magnificent, unique chapter of Church history came to a close. But the memory of the high and noble price that was paid for the Lord's house to "be established in the top of the mountains," as foretold by the prophet Isaiah, will never be forgotten.

List of Photographs and Illustrations

Much of the information for captions on pictures of the maritime vessels comes from Conway B. Sonne, *Ships, Saints, and Mariners*.

Cover. Louis, Paul, and Ejiler Nielsen. Courtesy of Archives Division, Historical Department, The Church of Jesus Christ of Latter-day Saints, Salt Lake City, Utah. Hereafter cited as LDS Church Archives.

Page 1. Valborg Rasmussen. Courtesy of Mona Lowe.

Page 3. Liverpool, England. Courtesy of S. George Ellsworth Photo Collection, Special Collections and Archives, Utah State University, Logan, Utah.

Page 4. The *Etna*. Courtesy of Peabody Essex Museum, Salem, Massachussets.

Page 7. The *Manhattan*. Courtesy of San Francisco Maritime NHP, Fireman's Fund.

Page 9. Folmer, Arnie, and Paul Jorgensen. Courtesy of LDS Church Archives.

Page 10. Woodcut of departing emigrants. Courtesy of The Church of Jesus Christ of Latter-day Saints Museum of Church History and Art. Hereafter cited as LDS Church History Museum.

Page 11. James Thomas Sutton and child. Courtesy of Thelma S. Anderson.

Page 12. The *Hudson*. Courtesy of The Mariners' Museum, Newport News, Virginia.

References

Allen, James B. and Thomas G. Alexander. *Manchester Mormons: The Journal of William Clayton.* Santa Barbara and Salt Lake City: Peregrine Smith, 1974.

Allen, Thomas William Frederick. Autobiography. In *The Allen Family,* by Mary Afton Allen Harker, 69–70. Idaho Falls, Idaho: Printcraft Press, 1966. Archives Division, Historical Department, The Church of Jesus Christ of Latter-day Saints, Salt Lake City, Utah.

Hereafter cited as LDS Church Archives.

Alston, Christopher. Autobiography. In *Our Pioneer Heritage,* 20 vols. compiled by Kate B. Carter, 8:36. Salt Lake City: Daughters of Utah Pioneers, 1965.

Atkin, Thomas. Autobiography. Holograph. LDS Church Archives.

Aveson, Mary Ann Rawlings. Reminiscences. In *A History of the Richard Rawlings Family,* compiled by Gladys

Rawlings Lemmon. Privately printed, 1986.

Ballard, Margaret McNeil. Autobiography. Holograph. Utah State Historical Society, Salt Lake City, Utah.

Beazer, Ellen Burton. Autobiography. In *Our Pioneer Heritage,* compiled by Kate B. Carter, 10:50–51. Salt Lake City: Daughters of Utah Pioneers, 1967.

Bennett, Emma Neat. Autobiography. In *Our Legacy from William and Elizabeth New,* compiled by

Archibald F. and Nordgren Blanche Bennett, 335–37. Privately printed, 1984. LDS Church Archives.

Bodily, Robert. Journal. Typescript. Utah State Historical Society.

Bradfield, William Henry. Reminiscences. In *Treasures of Pioneer History,* compiled by Kate B. Carter, vol. 3. Salt Lake City: Daughters of Utah Pioneers, 1954.

Carter, Sarah Davis. Autobiography. In *Our Pioneer Heritage,* compiled by Kate B. Carter, vol. 12. Salt Lake City: Daughters of Utah Pioneers, 1969.

Crane, Henry. Autobiography. In *Our Pioneer Heritage,* compiled by Kate B. Carter, 19:409–10. Salt Lake City: Daughters of Utah Pioneers, 1976.

Crouch, Ebenezer. Autobiography. Typescript. LDS Church Archives.

Cunningham, George. Reminiscenses. LDS Church Archives.

Davis, Mary M. Fretwell. Autobiography. LDS Church Archives.

Eccles, Bertha Marie Jensen. Autobiography. In *Utah Pioneer Biographies,"* 9:24–26, 28. Family History Library of The Church of Jesus Christ of Latter-day Saints, Salt Lake City, Utah. Hereafter cited as LDS Family History Library.

Ence, Gottlieb. "A Short Sketch of My Life." 1840–1918. LDS Church Archives.

Evans, Ruth Blair. Autobiography. "Utah Pioneer Biographies," 9:89–91, 93.

Fox, Ruth May. Autobiography. Typescript. LDS Church Archives.

Foxley, Grace Evans McLachlan. "Biographical Sketch of Charlotte Jarrold Hyder Evans," 1967. LDS Church Archives.

Frantzen, John. Reminiscences and Journal. LDS Church Archives.

Fry, John James. Journal. LDS Church Archives.

Green, Pearl Jacobs. "Brief history of Henry Peter Jacobs." In Maxine L. Breinholt, Biographies. LDS Church Archives.

Hafen, Mary Ann Stucki. *Recollections of a Handcart Pioneer of 1860: With Some Account of Frontier Life in* *Utah and Nevada.* Denver: privately printed, 1938.

"History of Henry Bolton and Mary Jane Smith." Typescript. In possession of Carol Bekker, Hyde Park, Utah.

"History of Sarah Ann Horsley." Autobiography. Typescript. In possession of Vicki Huish, Hyrum, Utah.

Jaques, John. Letter. Latter-day Saints' *Millennial Star* 18:26. 411–13. June 28, 1856.

Jenson, Andrew. *History of the Scandinavian Mission.* Salt Lake City: Deseret News Press, 1927.

Jenson, Olof. Autobiographical sketch. Typescript. LDS Church Archives.

Johnson, Ann Jane Willden. Autobiography. In *Our Pioneer Heritage,* compiled by Kate B. Carter, 13:231. Salt Lake City: Daughters of Utah Pioneers, 1970.

Journal of John Johnson Davies. Typescript. LDS Church Archives.

Latter-day Saints Millennial Star, 1840–1890. Liverpool, England.

Lindsay, James. Autobiography. Typescript. Utah State Historical Society.

Lindsay, William. Autobiography. Holograph. LDS Church Archives.

Lowder, Emily Hodgetts. Autobiography. In *Our Pioneer Heritage,* compiled by Kate B. Carter, vol. 7. Salt Lake City: Daughters of Utah Pioneers, 1964.

Mace, Mary Ann Greenhalgh. Autobiography. In *Our Pioneer Heritage,* compiled by Kate B. Carter, 15:125–27. Salt Lake City: Daughters of Utah Pioneers, 1972.

Madsen, Andrew. Autobiography. Typescript. LDS Church Archives.

Manfull, Emma Palmer. Autobiography. In "Utah Pioneer Biographies," 19:154–55. LDS Family History Library.

McBride, Heber Robert. Autobiography. Typescript. LDS Church Archives.

McCune, Elizabeth Grace. Autobiographical Sketch. In *Autobiography and Diaries of Frederick Henry McCune,* 19–21. LDS Church Archives.

Morris, Mary Lois Walker. Reminiscences. In *Our Pioneer Heritage,* compiled by Kate B. Carter, 12:450. Salt Lake City: Daughters of Utah Pioneers, 1969.

Moulton, Jensine Marie Jensen. In "History of a polygamist wife in Heber Valley. . . ." LDS Church Archives.

Moyle, James. Autobiography. Typescript. LDS Church Archives.

Mulder, William. *Homeward to Zion.* Minneapolis: University of Minnesota Press, 1957.

Norton, Maren Jensen Cutler. Autobiographical Sketch. In *Ancestry and Descendants of Mads Christian Jensen, 1600–1960,* compiled by Kathryn S. Jensen, 48–49. Privately printed. LDS Church Archives.

Olsen, Annie Catherine Christensen. Autobiography. In *"Utah Pioneer Biographies,"* 22:17–18, 20. LDS Family History Library.

Ottesen, Larsine Olsen. Autobiography. In *Our Pioneer Heritage,* compiled by Kate B. Carter, 17:167–68. Salt Lake City: Daughters of Utah Pioneers, 1974.

Palmer, Louisa Harriett Mills. Autobiography. In *Our Pioneer Heritage* compiled by Kate B. Carter, 13:455–57. Salt Lake City: Daughters of Utah Pioneers, 1970.

Pay, Mary Goble. Autobiography. Typescript. LDS Church Archives.

Personal History of James Horrace Skinner. Typescript. In private possession of Rohn (sic) Brown, Salt Lake City, UT.

Quayle, Thomas. Autobiography. In *Our Pioneer Heritage,* compiled by Kate B. Carter, 16:491–92. Salt Lake City: Daughters of Utah Pioneers, 1973.

Richardson, Agnes C. Hefferan. "Hefferan story," 10–12. LDS Church Archives.

Salmon, Margaret Robertson. Autobiography. In *Our Pioneer Heritage,* comp. by Kate B. Carter, vol. 11. Salt Lake City: Daughters of Utah Pioneers, 1968.

Simons, Fanny Fry. In *An Enduring Legacy,* vol. 6:187. Salt Lake City: Daughters of Utah Pioneers, 1983.

Sonne, Conway B. *Saints on the Seas: A Maritime History of Mormon Migration*

1830–1890. Salt Lake City: University of Utah Press, 1983.

Sonne, Conway B. *Ships, Saints, and Mariners: A Maritime Encyclopedia of Mormon Migration.* Salt Lake City: University of Utah Press, 1987.

Sorensen, Isaac. Journal. Special Collections and Archives, Utah State University, Logan, Utah.

Sprague, Martha Olson. Reminiscences. In "Utah Pioneer Biographies," 27:51–52. LDS Family History Library.

Steed, Thomas. Autobiography. *The Life of Thomas Steed from His Own Diary, 1826–1910.* LDS Church Archives.

Stevens, Augusta Dorius. Autobiography. Utah State Historical Society.

Stewart, Elizabeth White. Autobiography. In *Barnard White Family Book,* edited by Ruth Johnson and Glen F. Harding, 187, 189. Privately printed, 1967. LDS Church Archives.

Symons, Charles William. Autobiography. In *The Family of Charles William Symons and Arzella Whitaker Symons,* by Carley Budd Meridith and Dean Symons Anderson, 4–6. Privately printed, 1986. LDS Church Archives.

Taylor, P. A. M. *Expectations Westward, The Mormons and the Emigration of Their British Converts in the Nineteenth Century.* Ithaca, New York: Cornell University Press, 1966.

Tullidge, Edward W., *The Women of Mormondom,* 288. Salt Lake City, 1975.

Originally published in New York in 1877.

Vincent, Mary Ellison. Autobiography. LDS Church Archives.

Warner, Mary Ann Chapple. Autobiography. Typescript. Utah State Historical Society.

White, Thomas Henry. Autobiography. LDS Church Archives.

Winters, Johanna Kirstine Larsen. Autobiography. *Our Pioneer Heritage,* compiled by Kate B. Carter, vol. 11. Salt Lake City: Daughters of Utah Pioneers, 1968.

Wright, George. Letters, 1860. Holograph. LDS Church Archives.

Zollinger, Jacob. Autobiography. Holograph. Utah State University Special Collections and Archives, Logan, Utah.

Index